"*Sacred Leadership* clearly defines a new approach to leadership. The book not only outlines the theory behind the Sacred Leadership model, but also uses real life examples to ensure that it can be applied by anyone in a leadership position."

Andrew Lower, Executive Director
The Eleos Foundation

"*Sacred Leadership,* in an era where there is no clear definition between management and leadership, really opens up your eyes. Jim Davis is a common sense person who is a natural leader. If this country is to be saved from mediocrity, it's going to take leaders that place their efforts for the greater good over their personal career ladders. *Sacred Leadership* is a must read for anyone who wants to lead in the right direction and has the guts to do what is right."

Mark M. Skvarna
Superintendent, Baldwin Park
Unified School District

"Jim Davis has taken his thoughts and experiences and spoken directly to the heart of a mother who believes in his concepts of *Sacred Leadership* and as an advocate for the lesbian, gay, bisexual and transgender community. I loved his personal stories and was absolutely drawn into the content of the book. I believe that *Sacred Leadership* can raise the awareness of people from all walks of life, creating a world filled with more compassion, courage and community."

Marsha Aizumi, Author
Two Spirits, One Heart

*"Through the use of compelling stories and personal reflection, Mr. Davis challenges us to focus our energy and lead through purposeful mission and core institutional values. **Sacred Leadership's** authenticity inspires us to be mindful of the greatest good and the human needs of our constituencies. The principles set forth, provide a guide to assist us in making wiser and more informed decisions. This book is a must read for all leaders – it unleashes a passion for integrity and opens the door for possibilities."*

Elizabeth D. Jones, President
Institute for Educational Advancement

S A C R E D

Leading for the Greatest Good

LEADERSHIP

JAMES W. DAVIS

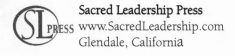

Sacred Leadership Press
www.SacredLeadership.com
Glendale, California

Cover Design:
David M. Geftakys

Cover Image:
quavondo/the Agency Collection/Getty Images

Interior Design:
Concepts Unlimited
www.ConceptsUnlimitedInc.com

ISBN-13: 978-0-98550-410-6 (pbk)
12   13   14   15   16   0 9 8 7 6 5 4 3 2 1

First Printing, 2012
Printed in the United States of America

DEDICATION

To my parents...

TABLE OF CONTENTS

ACKNOWLEDGEMENTS

There are many people who influenced the development and writing of this book. First and foremost I honor my parents, Nelle and Emerson Davis. Neither lived to see its publication but their influence was instrumental in shaping me and my values as a leader.

I offer a special thanks to my wife, Judy, for her persistence and support over my years of researching, writing and editing. She has read and commented on more drafts, many unreadable, than any human being should have to endure.

More broadly I honor the many leaders, teachers, parents and students who taught me so much in my nearly 30-year career in public education. Literally, hundreds of colleagues supported and influenced me. However, the following people powerfully influenced my view and practice of leadership: Paul Possemato, Jim Taylor, Walker Carlton, John Howard and Harry Handler. They were role models and mentors at crucial periods in my career.

I also want to recognize three of the teachers who greeted me in the cafeteria at John Adams Junior High and became friends and mentors as I was thrown into the chaos of inner city Los Angeles: Glenn "Pete" Peters, Corky Matsumoto and Bob Walton.

Many people have provided advice, support and editorial comment over the years. Marsha Aizumi, Carol Barkley, Rick Brush, Cynthia Cavalli, Mike Coppess, Jaci Doer, William Durden, Kathryn de Planque, David Geftakys, Erika Jacobi, Elizabeth Jones, Sue Kagel, Pete Lakey, Michael Laney, Ksenia Lauren, Andy and Jessica Lower, Jeffrey McCausland, Michael Piechowski, Pat and Tom Ressler, Meredith and Tom Reynolds, Mark Skvarna, Chiara Tellini and

Richard and Sherry Vaughan. Special thanks also go to Robert Yehling of Word Journeys for helping me find my writer's voice and for early editorial assistance.

The old maxim that I "stand on the shoulders of giants" applies to the writing of this book. The book draws from my experience, my reading, my interactions with tens of thousands of people in the schools I worked in and led, as well as the companies with which I have consulted. I have read the works of hundreds of authors and interacted with many experts and leaders in the writing of this book. I have attempted to give credit and attribution throughout the book recognizing their contributions to my story.

I corrected errors in spelling and grammar within quotes rather than using brackets. These changes did not alter the speaker's or writer's meaning. Full citations for all quotes can be found in the End Notes and should be referenced by those who wish to use these quotes.

I have attempted to name important mentors and sources within the book but for the sake of readability I was not able to include everyone. Those names appear in this Acknowledgement or in the End Notes.

PREFACE

Our time requires leadership that has moved beyond short-term personal self-interest to a long-term view with global human interests at its heart. We need leadership that transcends the "common good" and recognizes that there is a "greatest good" that serves a humanity not defined by country, state, city or tribe – but by our interconnectedness.[1] It is leadership that acknowledges we are all part of the same whole, linked together through a series of interdependent relationships. This type of leadership understands and recognizes what is sacred within and between us individually and collectively.

I call this *Sacred Leadership*.

This is a time of extraordinary urgency that calls for leaders who care about something greater than themselves. It is time to reconnect with our sacred purpose as human beings.

The book is written for those in the service professions, public servants, business owners, corporate executives and parents.

Service Professions

First it is directed at those dedicating their lives to professions that serve the greatest good. There are many such professions, including education, health care, firefighting, law enforcement, social work, law, journalism and many more. There are also the many nonprofits that serve a variety of needs in our society. I call these the "sacred professions." By this, I do not mean religious professions, or faith-based organizations, though if their missions are sound, they certainly belong. These professions are sacred by virtue of their missions to serve the public good. These career paths exist to educate, nurture, heal or protect our fellow human beings. Ideally, the missions of these professions are powerful and deeply rooted in service to the larger society.

These sacred professions and institutions occupy a unique, but important, place in our American democracy and in the larger global community. We have always been a fiercely independent people, but from the beginning, our forbearers realized that we must care for one another if our democracy is to survive.

Public Servants

This book is also written for public servants, especially those who hold elected office. In today's sound bite driven news cycle, it requires great moral courage (or a huge ego or craving for power) for anyone to enter the political arena. Once there, they are exposed to what authors and columnists Mark Heilemann and Mark Halperin call "the combination meat grinder/flesh incinerator that postmodern politics has become."[2] Our political process has always been messy, but today it has become cruel and dysfunctional. It absolutely needs to change if we are to realize our potential as a force for peace and progress in the world.

The stakes are far too consequential to ignore the higher principles of the greatest good. If our political leaders will not rise above their partisan, and often silly, arguments and take on the issues that impact the greatest good, we will become a mere shadow of our promise.

Business and Corporate Leaders

It has become clear that the message of *Sacred Leadership* also applies to the corporate, for-profit sector as well. There is some reason for optimism in this area. In a 2005 Boston College survey, 91% of surveyed senior executives in large corporations believed that the public has a right to expect good corporate citizenship.[3] A follow-up study in 2009, following the great recession, found that "Despite upheaval in the economy, a majority of U.S. companies are not making major changes in corporate citizenship practices...Most U.S. senior executives believe business should be more involved than it is today in addressing major public issues including health care, product safety, education and climate change."[4] Although business leaders must keep their eye on shareholder value and the financial health of their companies, many also recognize that a growing 21st Century society demands responsible corporate citizenship on a global scale. The *Los Angeles Times* reported that seven states have passed legislation forming "benefit corporations." These laws "allow companies to officially adopt policies that 'create a material positive impact on society and the environment' as an integral part of their charters."[5]

Sacred Leadership has become even more important in corporate boardrooms because of corporations' new and unprecedented ability to shape laws and regulations. In January of 2010, the United States Supreme Court decision in *Citizens United v. Federal Election Commission*[6] granted First Amendment rights to free speech to corporations. This ruling gave corporations the ability to use their billions in profits to fund political speech in order to influence the political process. In effect, the Supreme Court said that corporations are people in the context of the First Amendment right to free speech.

There was a time when government represented the people; when it looked out for their well-being by providing infrastructure, education and general support in difficult times. That contract with the people is now about to be broken unless leaders at all levels recognize, understand and act on their responsibility to the greatest good.

Parents

Although I do not address parents specifically in this book, its message is also meant for them. The fundamentals of *Sacred Leadership* begin the day a child is born. These include a commitment to greater purpose, a foundation of humane values and respect for the law, responsibility for the present and accountability for the future. These fundamental principles certainly rang true for me while I was growing up in a small town and in a small family business. My parents made sure of it; they instilled these values in me every day. Parents should be the most fundamental practitioners of *Sacred Leadership* in our society. They must continue to rise to the challenge and make the necessary and difficult sacrifices required by the most sacred of all responsibilities – the raising and nurturing of our youth.

In the pages that follow, we will explore the principles of *Sacred Leadership*, as well as the personal skills and attributes it requires.

I offer this book to those leaders who are connecting or reconnecting to the greater purpose in their leadership practice, the "sacred" aspects of their work. You are the leaders who inspire me in my work and moved me to pick up pen and paper to write this book.

"Sacred – Unassailable, inviolable, highly valued and important" [7]

Chapter 1

THE SACRED IN "SACRED" LEADERSHIP

Over the years, I found it difficult to articulate the kind of leadership I envisioned. Then, one night while I was lying in bed, it came to me. The work I was doing was "sacred." My experiences as an educator taught me that I was doing something very important – not only for the students with whom I worked, but also for the future of our country and humanity. Nurturing and educating young people are sacred callings, not in a religious sense, but rather in the level of importance we ascribe to the work. That was it – *Sacred Leadership!*

As I enthusiastically shared this insight, I received a tepid, if not hostile, response. My non-religious friends and colleagues had difficulty separating sacred from its religious context, and those who were religious couldn't understand how something sacred was not tied to their particular religious beliefs.

However, as I explained my rationale, they got it, and none could come up with a better term that actually described the concept I was talking about. So, *Sacred Leadership* stuck.

> *Sacred Leadership* is defined by missions that recognize and value what is sacred to humankind and that serve the greatest good.

What is Sacred?

By sacred I mean missions that serve the greatest good; missions that educate, nurture, heal or protect; missions so powerful and deeply rooted in service to the larger community that their rightness is indisputable.

Sacred Leadership is not about religion or any other organized belief system or ideology. Donah Zohar, a management thought leader, talks of drawing upon "...deeper nonsectarian meanings, values, purposes and motivations that might be sacred to any human being."[8] Deep inside us is something greater, something that rises up beyond self-interest to serving the greatest good. No one person, religion or belief system can magically transport us through these chaotic and perilous times. Only a focus on what is sacred in our lives and in our work will allow us to create a livable world today and a positive world tomorrow through our combined and cooperative efforts to identify and serve the greatest good.

An amazing example was recently called to my attention – a documentary entitled *Boatlift*,[9] produced to honor the tenth anniversary of the 9/11 terrorist attacks in New York and Washington D.C. The story that follows gives life to my meaning of sacred.

Boatlift

The largest boatlift in history occurred on 9/11 (greater than the one at Dunkirk during World War II) when volunteers in hundreds of boats, and with no planning, evacuated nearly 500,000 New Yorkers from Lower Manhattan in less than nine hours.

On seeing the thousands of New Yorkers crowding onto the piers and seawalls in Lower Manhattan, Michael Day, Commander of the United States Coast Guard Pilot Boat #1 put out a radio call, "All available boats, anyone that wants to help with the evacuation of Lower Manhattan, report to Governor's Island." He did not know if anyone would respond to his call for help. Yet, within 20 minutes there were boats all across the horizon, hundreds of boats converging on Lower Manhattan. "If it floated, and it could get there, it got there," Robin Jones, engineer of the tugboat, *Mary Gellatly*, recalled.

The captains and crew of this fleet of boats came together with no idea what they would be getting into and no idea whether Manhattan, or even their own boats, might be attacked in the next few hours. All they knew was that desperate people were in need of help and they couldn't turn their backs on them, even if that meant putting their own lives at risk.

Perhaps one of the most amazing aspects of this mass-scale operation was that there were no evacuation plans for such a rescue. "You couldn't have planned anything to happen that fast that quick," Jones said.

Each of these individuals practiced *Sacred Leadership* that day. They identified and served a greater purpose, coming to the aide of nearly 500,000 people. They also illustrated that leadership can emerge from any position, be it that of a Coast Guard Commander or the captain of a party boat.

The Power of the Sacred

What took nine days at Dunkirk, took nine hours in lower Manhattan on September 11. It is not a coincidence that the response of the boatmen produced a powerful result that day. When leaders tap into sacred purpose, they act from a different place and with a different energy. The sacred nature of their work sustains them through physical and emotional exhaustion, stress and doubt. Let me share an example from my personal experience.

From Broken Heart to Open Heart

In the early 1980s I was assigned as the Dean at Belmont High

School, in inner city Los Angeles. The school served nearly 4,500 low-income, immigrant students in a multi-story prison-like building on less than ten acres of land. The students came from around the world, speaking over 80 languages. Walking through the halls one experienced a blur of languages and cultures and I often felt that I had been transported to the United Nations! These students came to Belmont with hopes and dreams of a better life. Almost everyone who worked there saw themselves not only as educators but also as nurturers of dreams. Their work went beyond reading, writing and arithmetic to the sacred calling of the profession.

One of those students was Francisco, a wonderful, outgoing young man full of life and fun. During his study hall, Francisco volunteered as a Spanish language translator in my office. He had come from El Salvador with his mother to escape the violence and bloodshed there. I took Francisco under my wing and quickly became a father figure. He would drop by the office after school and just talk about what was going on in his life – family, school, work, girls and dreams of college. My role moved beyond educating, to nurturing and supporting this wonderful human being.

Unbelievably, while visiting a next door neighbor, he was gunned down by a pimp who thought Francisco was moving into his territory. I'll never forget raising money for his funeral and taking it to his grieving mother. A young life full of possibility was snuffed out in an instant. He was not just another random victim of violence; he was a friend, a son, a future possibility never to be realized.

Losing Francisco broke my heart. As difficult as his loss was, I was able to move from a broken heart to an open heart by recommitting to the sacred nature of my work, feeling strongly and passionately about the huge difference I could make in the lives of my students and their families.

Francisco's death was not an exception. During my nearly 30

years as a leader in the public schools, I experienced a great deal of joy and satisfaction, but also a lot of pain. Tragically, I mourned the loss of nearly 50 young people – all students of mine. A few died of natural causes and others from drugs, accidents or suicide, but most perished from the gang and random criminal violence that ripped through the inner core of Los Angeles.

Like Francisco, all of the young people I have lost, left an indelible mark deep in my heart, not only as a person but as a leader. These experiences forged my conviction to accept nothing short of *Sacred Leadership* in both my personal life and my professional life.

Secular versus Sacred

Experiences like the one with Francisco do not always lead to a reconnection and recommitment to sacred purpose. Often, people can't move beyond their broken heart and they withdraw into the drudgery of their work, disconnecting themselves from the sacred part of their mission. Others never connect to the sacred from the beginning. These are the people who say, "I teach subject matter, not kids."

Another part of the disconnect from the sacred nature of our work can be attributed to a purely secular approach found in all aspects of our professional lives. As futurist Eamonn Kelly points out, "The secular mindset…is the outcome of a deeper philosophical shift in which reason supplanted belief as the central maker and organizer of meaning…."[10] The secular mindset dominates our view of human activity, leaving no room for our spiritual need to connect to higher purpose. This mindset still permeates our approach to education, health care and most other professions and businesses in this country.

The move to a secular mindset has both positive and negative consequences. Certainly the rationality of the Enlightenment continues to deeply influence western thought. It has brought not only economic success but also, as Kelly goes on to say, "principles and ideals that people in the developed world take for granted today… democracy, freedom, individual liberty and tolerance of differing belief systems are all offspring of secular modernity."[11] However, we have allowed our rationality to dominate, disconnecting us from sacred purpose and what makes us human.

A Blended Approach

I am not, however, advocating a return to religiosity in our political and professional lives. Just as the purely secular approach has failed to serve the future, a strident religious stance is interfering with our ability to succeed in this new global environment.

Throughout history we have seen the negative consequences of mixing the religious with the political. The Roman Inquisition, the Crusades and the tragedy of 9/11 all highlight the danger in mixing politics and religious fundamentalism. There was a reason that our founding fathers included a separation of church and state in the Constitution.

There is a different way to wed the positive aspects of the secular approach with a higher spiritual purpose. It recognizes our interconnectedness and interdependence. That new way is *Sacred Leadership*.

Sacred Purpose as a Global Positioning System (GPS) for Leaders

Because of our interconnectedness and interdependence, we are living in a time of choice like no other in the history of humankind.[12] It is easy to lose our way. The choices we make today will determine whether we reach our promise as a species, or simply pass the way of the dinosaur. This is uncharted territory in which we face unprecedented complexity and chaos. It is no longer enough to simply consult a new map. It must be a different kind of map drawn from a different vision – a "seeing" that recognizes a sacred mission to serve the greatest good.

In these complex and chaotic times, we must resist the tendency to revert to our basic instinct of "fight or flight" which is ineffective at best and destructive in most cases. *Sacred Leadership* has a built-in GPS by which we engage ourselves and others at a higher plane – a more sacred plane. That GPS is found in the sacred nature of our mission, and once referenced, enables us to face fear, anxiety and multiple unknowns with a different feeling, a sense of sure purpose derived from serving the greatest good. This connection and commitment to sacred purpose also leads to increased personal and organizational responsibility and accountability.

Sacred Leadership:
Connecting the Mind, Heart and Hand

Sacred missions touch the core of what makes us human. Our abilities to connect empathically, to care deeply and to serve others, feed the ever-compassionate heart of *Sacred Leadership*.

As we serve others through our focus on a larger purpose, both parties undergo a transformation. In serving the greatest good, one's heart and soul are awakened and strengthened. We gain a more expansive, clearer view of the big picture and the impact of our actions on large groups of people and all of humanity. This awareness elevates our level of consciousness, creating a greater commitment to the work and becoming the driving force behind our actions. Thus, *Sacred Leadership* not only transforms the institution and those it serves, but, more importantly, it transforms each of us individually at a deep interior level. We begin to recognize our interconnectedness to each other as well as to our planet as a whole.

In the practice of *Sacred Leadership* your very being begins to change. You approach both the present and future with an open mind, heart and will. To do this requires a new way of seeing, feeling and doing.[13]

The leader sees differently, unburdened by the past, and the old way of viewing things. The leader suspends judgment and maintains a mind open to new ideas, possibilities and points of view.

The leader feels differently, releasing cynicism and embracing the world with love by maintaining an open heart, as I did after Francisco's death. Rather than succumb to cynicism and withdraw, the leader engages and opens his or her heart to deeper understanding and the sacred nature of the mission.

Finally, the leader acts differently, first by letting go of fear and then realigning with the mission to serve the greatest good; thus tapping back into the power and energy needed to see, feel and do anew. By fear I am referring to that voice in the head that often appears just as we are ready to act. It presents itself saying: "You can't succeed!" "You are incapable!" "You don't know what you are doing!" When we listen to that negative inner voice, we step away from the future that is about to emerge and find ourselves falling backwards into the past – past behaviors, past patterns, past heartaches, past disappointments and past failures.[14] Letting go of fear allows us to take action and move forward into new possibilities.

At the Core

So the question becomes how do we take action and move forward? Most of the discussion about leadership today focuses on the individual **leader**, or what I call the cult of personality.

In contrast, *Sacred Leadership* focuses on an abiding purpose or **mission**, guided by *values* in order to serve the **greatest good** with a present and *future* view. In other words, it is about the purpose or mission – not the person. These principles describe a kind of *leadership*, not a kind of leader.

> One does **not** become a sacred leader;
> rather one becomes a leader who practices
> **Sacred Leadership.**

The importance of the individual leader's personal attributes and skills becomes relevant only in the context of his or her ability to serve the mission.

In summary, leadership is sacred when it:

- Focuses on a mission to serve the greatest good;
- Is guided by enduring values (such as trust, respect, compassion and integrity) and the democratic rule of law;
- Enlists, engages and sustains others in the possibilities inherent in the mission;
- Meets the needs of the present, *and* provides for the future.

We'll explore each of these in more detail in the following chapters.

Chapter 1 Questions for Reflection

1. What provides deep meaning in your life?

2. Of those things that have deep meaning, which would you describe as sacred as the term is explained in this chapter?

3. What is the sacred nature of your work?

4. How do you model that sacred nature in your daily actions as a leader (understanding that we lead at all times)?

"There is no history;
only biography" [15]

—Ralph Waldo Emerson

Chapter 2

MY STORY

There are those of us in leadership positions who are asking, "Why are we leading? What is the greater purpose in what we do? Will this all matter when I leave this job or am gone from this life?"

Many of our institutions, both private and public, have shifted their attention away from truly caring for their products, customers and communities, to following the business principles of hyper competition. They have trained their cross-hairs on market share and profits. These management practices have also found their way into the public and non-profit sectors where conversations more often focus on efficiency and revenue streams rather than on the mission or service to be delivered. While the application of good management principles is essential to our stewardship of public, non-profit and private resources, the focus on purely financial outcomes has blurred our sense of mission and our values-driven commitment to serve something larger than ourselves. We have mistaken management for leadership.

Something has been lost along the way. Our sense of deeper purpose, that innate desire or need to make a difference and contribute to a larger good, has been subordinated to the never-ending effort to improve the bottom line. Unfortunately, this connection to greater purpose is often considered an intangible, something that cannot be measured or quantified. Thus, institutions often throw it on the back burner – or eliminate it completely.

Certainly, our experiences with corporate, non-profit and government mismanagement and malfeasance over the past decade (Hurricane Katrina, services for the poor being cut, schools closing, Enron, Tyco, AIG, Shearson Lehman Brothers, the tech bubble, the collapse of the banking industry and housing market, GM, etc.) have shown us that managing for the short-term gain of CEOs and shareholders will not lead to personal fulfillment or economic prosperity because it is the spiritual nature of our work that drives us to greatness.

Sacred Leadership offers a different path that reconnects us to our sacred purpose as human beings and honors our interdependence and interconnectedness.

Sacred Leadership is the result of a long personal journey that began in a small town in Ohio, continued into the inner city of Los Angeles and led to the board rooms of non-profit and for-profit companies.

I began my first teaching job in 1970, a short time after the race riots of the 1960s, a time when anger and helplessness still seethed below the surface in America's inner cities. For nearly 20 years, I worked in many of the toughest areas of Los Angeles in positions that ranged from teacher to high school principal. I served with hundreds of teachers and school administrators, some very successful, others abject failures. Almost all the administrators were good managers; they ran safe schools (especially compared to the neighborhoods in which they were situated), made sure kids attended class, hired teachers, balanced budgets, and oversaw modest gains in student achievement.

As I look back, what separated the good from the bad was *leadership*. It was not about some bigger than life charismatic leader we so often see portrayed in the media. In fact, some of the best leaders I worked with were often the least charismatic. These special few were driven by a great purpose. They saw beyond the need for good management (which is required) to their sacred purpose of nurturing and educating their charges. They saw their students not as commodities in a factory called school, but rather as valuable and unique individuals who would shape the future. With that awareness, they could not let themselves fail.

This book describes how I came to the idea of *Sacred Leadership* and how it evolved to become the way I coach business executives, educators and other professionals, as well as the way I conduct my consulting practice and my personal life.

It is in this context that I offer my story.

Xenia, Ohio Meets Inner-City Los Angeles

I grew up in Xenia, Ohio, a typical, small midwest town that was primarily a working class community. In the 60s, during the height of the racial tensions gripping the rest of the nation, our town quietly and voluntarily integrated its schools. There were no protests, boycotts or violence. The process was not perfect, but for the most part, black and white kids got along well.

My parents owned a neighborhood grocery store that had been in the family for three generations. My great-grandfather first opened the store in the late 1800s. It was about the same size as a 7-Eleven but carried a full range of groceries, fresh produce and featured a full-service meat counter. I began working there when I was five years old, acquiring a strong work ethic and the sense that I was to be a responsible citizen.

In this setting, at the age of six or seven, I began to understand that we had a responsibility to serve something greater than ourselves. It is a lesson my father taught me.

Every week I watched with great curiosity as some of the customers, usually men, came into the store and talked with my father.

After some discussion, they signed a piece of paper and, without paying, left with a bag or two of groceries. As I grew older, I realized that my father kept a small file box for these pieces of paper. When a family fell on hard times, he gave them groceries for the week, recorded the amount and filed it in that box he kept under the counter. A week or two later, those same customers would return to see my father again and pay him. He tore up that piece of paper. No interest was charged, but a lot of good will was gained and our neighbors were able to eat. No one went hungry.

When I questioned my father, he told me this practice started with his grandfather and was continued on by his father and now our family. "Serving our neighbors," he said, "even when it was hard on us, was the right thing to do."

My parents were both high school graduates. My mother came from a very humble background on a farm. Both of her parents were orphaned; neither had an education beyond the third grade. My mother was determined that my sister and I attend college. When the time came, off we went.

That decision to go to college meant I was not going to take over the grocery. That was fine with me because it was clear that we would not be able to compete with the big super market chains in the years ahead. For health reasons, my father sold our grocery store to my cousin, who ran it for several more years before it closed for good. It is now a vacant lot.

In college I majored in biology and chemistry and wanted to be a scientist. It may be difficult to understand in today's information age; but I knew no one in Xenia who could tell me how to be a scientist and I did not have an advisor to show me the direction when I got to college. It is hard to believe just how naïve I was but I didn't have a clue how to pursue my dream, so I chose to teach science instead. This decision led to a long journey of nearly 40 years in public service, during which the concept of *Sacred Leadership* evolved.

I graduated from college in June 1970 and signed a contract with the Los Angeles Unified School District two months later. I moved to California with my wife of one year and waited to be assigned my first teaching job. Within a month, I was concerned; I hadn't heard from the district since I signed the contract, even though the school year had begun. I kept calling. No response. Finally, about six weeks into the school year, someone discovered I was on the payroll but had not been assigned to a school. I was told to report to Griffith Junior High School in East Los Angeles.

The next morning, I got in my car at 6:00 a.m. and drove to my first teaching job. I was excited, nervous and full of expectations. I had completed my student teaching at Scottsdale High School, located in an upper middle class suburb of Phoenix. It wasn't much different than my small hometown of Xenia. The Scottsdale kids had more money, and drugs were more prevalent (after all, we were riding the tail end of the 1960s), but that was the only difference. The classrooms were basically the same.

As I drove to Griffith Junior High, I thought I knew what to expect. After all, just how different could things be?

I arrived at the school early. It was an older building, surrounded by a chain link fence. I found the faculty parking lot and made my way to the main office. The office was a flurry of activity, with adults, kids and parents scuttling everywhere. It felt like organized chaos, hectic but under control. The secretary asked what I wanted, not sure if I was a student or adult. I said I was a teacher and had been told to report.

"Well, no one told us," she said tersely. "Please take a seat over there." She pointed to a line of chairs against the wall.

I sat with the waiting parents and kids. About 30 minutes passed. The bell rang to start the school day. PA announcements were made and things calmed down. A man with a commanding presence walked into the room from the hallway. He spoke to the secretary, and then turned to me with a smile. "Hi, I am Paul Possemato, the principal. I apologize for your wait. No one told us you were coming! Please come into my office,"

I began to relax as I chatted with this capable and caring principal. Years later, he would become a professional friend and mentor.

I was assigned to Mr. Nelson, the head counselor, and an equally likeable man. His daily workload was certainly full enough without having me under foot, but he put me to work on clerical tasks. My morning finally gained some structure. In the afternoon, one of the teachers left (or walked out), and I was asked to cover his classes for the remainder of the day. The kids were restless and tested me, but the rest of the day went without fanfare. It wasn't an auspicious beginning to my career but finally I was working – I was a teacher!

I reported back to Griffith Junior High for one more day, and then received a call that gave me the choice of two teaching positions. One was a general science position at John Adams Junior High School in downtown Los Angeles, and the other was a biology position at Birmingham High School in the San Fernando Valley, a predominantly middle class area of the city. After I got home, I pulled out my map of Los Angeles. John Adams was much closer to my apartment (by nearly 25 miles), so I agreed to take that position.

Little did I know what a life-changing decision that would turn out to be! It was the first of many small decisions that led to major changes and shifts in my life's direction. Had I chosen Birmingham High School, I would have been teaching Biology and Chemistry to suburban kids and would never have had the many experiences described in this book.

The next morning, I headed down the freeway to central Los Angeles. The commute took over an hour, but I still arrived almost an hour before the school day began. I pulled off Interstate 10 and headed south on Broadway about 20 blocks. I saw nothing but concrete, warehouses, and small factories; hardly a tree or blade of grass stood anywhere. I wondered if I had missed the turn.

When I reached 28th Street, I saw the school. The first building was a two-story "temporary classroom" (which still exists today, four decades later), housed near an asphalt covered playground surrounded by the highest chain link fence I had ever seen. The main building was an old, dirty two-story beige schoolhouse. Across the street was an equally dismal playground and gymnasium, which I later found were connected to the main campus by two dark tunnels that ran under Broadway. I found a small parking lot and pulled in. I felt relieved that I could park there. I knew it couldn't be safe to leave my car on the street.

I walked into the building and found the main office. I introduced myself; this time, they were expecting me. "Welcome, Mr. Davis," the secretary said. She ushered me into the principal's office. Mr. Hahn was a tall, handsome man with an air of authority. He asked about my background and told me a bit about the school and my assignment. "You'll find your experience here very different from Scottsdale. Our school is 95% black and 4% Hispanic, with a few Asian kids mixed in. Almost all of our students are from very poor families, and many of their parents are illiterate. There is some holdover hostility from the riots that occurred in 1965, especially because the National Guard was stationed on our campus. Also, there are still some rifts in the faculty over the strike that occurred last year (1969)."

"Unfortunately, you will have three different subject preparations," he continued. "You will be teaching health, general science and basic math, and you will be traveling each period to a different classroom. I think you should also know that your classes have had six different teachers in as many weeks, so discipline is weak."

What an understatement! When I walked into my first classroom, I ran into full-throated, full-bodied chaos like I'd never seen before. Kids walked and ran across the top of the desks, the noise was so loud I couldn't hear myself think. One kid climbed the blinds; another hung from the second-story window. Paper flew across the room. My heart pounded in my head. I had never imagined a classroom or situation like this.

"Everyone sit down," I said.

No one heard me over the uproar. "SIT DOWN!" I shouted.

A few heads looked up, but the chaos continued. Then I saw a yardstick on the chalk tray. I picked it up and slapped it across the desk, making a loud sound. The room grew quiet. "Everyone in their seats!" My loud voice vibrated with an unfamiliar demand.

Most moved. A few didn't. I slapped down the yardstick again. "NOW!"

Finally, everyone complied. My heart wanted to burst from my chest. I felt like I was about to lose control of my own reality.

"Good morning, I am Mr. Davis, and I am going to be your teacher for the rest of the year,"

"Yeah, that's what the last six said," shouted a young man from the back of the room. Laughter broke out.

"I'm different – now let's get on with the lesson,"

That's when I realized there wasn't a lesson. I didn't know what book they were using or what, if anything, they had accomplished the first six weeks. The class started to shift and murmur, like a living beast with a mind of its own, rather than a room of 35 individual adolescents.

"We were working on addition and subtraction," a frail-voiced girl in the front row said.

"Thank you." I began to write problems on the chalk board.

Throughout the period, the kids tested me. I responded with a verbal force I'd never imagined being necessary in a classroom. This scene played out four more times as I started each new class, as both the kids and I ran breathlessly through the door to beat the tardy bell.

As I drove home at the end of the day, I asked aloud, "What the hell happened?" I wondered if I would return. *Could I return?*

When I got home, my wife, a surgical nurse, was at work. With no one to talk to, I walked into the bedroom and collapsed.

Bzzz, Bzzz...

The alarm sounded at 5:00 a.m. Within 45 minutes, I was up, showered and on my way to work. I got there at 6:30 a.m. I don't know why, but I figured someone would be on campus and could help me find some paper and other materials, and get some work-sheets together for the day.

I found my way to the teachers' cafeteria. Sitting around the table were four men drinking coffee, talking and laughing. I introduced myself and they laughed. "We thought you were a student," said a big, gray-haired black man.

Then the whole group laughed again. I was incredulous. I didn't get the joke that, since I was white, I couldn't have been a student at the school. I smiled and they said, "Sit down, let us buy you a cup of coffee,"

These veteran teachers took an interest in me, as had the principal at Griffith Junior High School. My life was about to change for the better. They took me to the workroom and showed me the ditto machine (this predecessor to modern copying machines produced blue copies that smelled like acetone). Another teacher offered math worksheets. I was set for the day. On my way out the door, one of the teachers said, "Remember Jim, don't smile 'til Christmas!"

A few days passed and things were only marginally better in the discipline category. It was a constant test of wills. There were many days when I was certain the kids would win. Besides the five academic classes, I was also assigned a homeroom to manage. I was responsible for 35 seventh grade boys in Homeroom B62. During this 15-minute period, I took attendance, read the daily bulletin and took care of other administrative issues. The boys in the classroom were squirrely, but as seventh graders, they were still somewhat intimidated by their transition to junior high school.

One morning I asked, "What does it take to make you kids behave?"

One of the kids smiled and said, "We'll tell you tomorrow,"

I was usually in my room early, with the door open, heating my coffee in a beaker over the Bunsen burner. Early the next morning, five boys came in and said, "Here's your answer, Mr. Davis."

They handed me a long wooden paddle with the inscription "Peace Maker" carved on one side and "Homeroom Number B62" carved on the other. The biggest said, "Just use this and we'll behave,"

I was shocked. In my childhood, I had never received more than a swat on my butt. Furthermore, I was a blazing antiwar peace activist (what the media and more conservative people would call a left-wing liberal today). "I don't even hit dogs." I said. "I am certainly not going to hit you kids,

They laughed and said, "Well you'd better learn to if you want some peace around here."

The next day, one of the boys in homeroom went too far. "Swat him!" the kids yelled.

I called up the young man in front of the class and told him to bend over. I gave him a good one across the rear. He said, "I am sorry Mr. Davis," with no anger or attitude.

Apparently, just the threat of the paddle, the knowledge that I could and would use corporal punishment, was all I needed. I only used the paddle one more time. One day, a boy named Larry was really acting up and pushing all of my buttons – including calling me profanities. I was angry! I took Larry outside and told him to bend over. With full force, I put the "Peace Maker" in motion. Larry moved and I missed my mark; the paddle struck his lower back. He screamed out and winced in pain, but fortunately it turned out he was OK. I don't know who was more terrified, Larry or me.

What was I doing? In trying to adapt to this new environment and culture, I had violated one of my basic values! After all, as I told the kids, "I don't even hit dogs,"

I never used the paddle again – nor did I need to.

The transition was not completed overnight. Students who gain bad habits and control over the classroom do not give ground easily, but at least some learning took place every day. I continued to drive home exhausted, and used every waking hour at home to plan lessons or complain to my wife. When we went out with our friends, I fell asleep at the dinner table. By the middle of my first year of teaching, my young marriage was over and my wife had left me.

Throughout the first semester, the four men I met in the cafeteria that first morning continued to support me and offer advice. I soon became the fifth teacher at that early morning table. After my wife left, the cafeteria manager made sure I received breakfast in the morning. Mr. Matsumoto, the teacher in the room next to mine, asked his wife to make an extra sandwich for my lunch. This community of strangers soon became friends and helped me through both professional and personal crises.

Mr. Matsumoto became a mentor to me. His real name was Minoru, but he went by Corky. His parents had been forced into one of the internment camps during World War II. In spite of this treatment, Corky went on to serve in the U.S. military during the Korean conflict. Talk about injustices! I was shocked that I had never been taught or even heard about these camps into which Japanese-American citizens had been forced. This sad chapter in the otherwise victorious U.S. World War II effort never appeared in my school history texts! As with my young charges, I learned that things are not always as they seem. I tried to judge less and see more clearly as the school year progressed.

During the second semester, I won the lottery, five new classes and my own classroom. My classroom preparations were reduced to general science and health. This time I knew "not to smile until Easter," and started my classes with a hopeful heart hidden behind an iron hand. I established discipline on day one and maintained it every second, driven by the constant fear I would lose control of this bunch.

Soon, Corky asked me to co-sponsor the science club. I began spending every Saturday hauling the kids out of the ghetto and into the mountains, beaches and deserts. It amazed me that most had never seen snow, the ocean or a cactus, even though they lived within an hour of the San Gabriel Mountains, Santa Monica Beach and Anza-Borrego Desert. As the year continued, I put together Corky's stories of the internment camp and my observations of these kids. The two converged into a realization: These kids lived in their own kind of "concentration camp," confined by poverty and the threat of gang violence.

On a day I will never forget, I was telling my science club about the University of Southern California (USC) and the Los Angeles County Natural History Museum, both located just a few blocks away. The vast majority looked at me with blank stares. It became clear that they had no idea what I was talking about! "Where's this great university?" they asked. As I described USC, they said, "Oh, that's across the freeway. That's Hoover Groover (a local gang) territory. We can't go there." This was the year before the Bloods and

Crips became household names, when the local gangs still controlled neighborhood areas.

Once again, the proverbial scales fell from my eyes and I saw even more clearly. That next Saturday, we all piled into our cars with the kids and off we went to the university and the museum. Twenty kids' lives changed for the better.

• • • • •

Later that year, the issue of gang violence struck home in a very personal way. The day had just begun when one of my homeroom boys started banging on my classroom door and shouting, "Mr. Davis, Mr. Davis, Let me in!" (In those days, as today, we kept our doors locked for security reasons.)

I opened the door. A group of about thirty young men hovered in the courtyard below, menacing looks on their faces. I pulled the student inside and shut the door. "What's going on!"

"They are going to kill me!"

I told my student aide to pass through the workroom and alert the other science teachers. I grabbed a baseball bat that I carried for playground duty and went outside, ordering my class to stay put and be quiet. As I walked down the outdoor stairs, teachers from the science and PE departments joined me. All had heard that there was trouble.

We began to chase the gang off campus. As the gang members climbed the fence to exit, we turned to head back to our classrooms.

Without warning, one of the gangbangers jumped off the fence, ran up behind me and hit me on the back of my head. I turned and saw a young man in a purple, sleeveless shirt run and jump the fence. The chase began. I never lost sight of that purple shirt. I chased him seven blocks to the side of the Harbor Freeway, caught him and, in that moment, was ready to bash in his head with my bat. Fortunately, hands suddenly grabbed my shoulders and two police officers pulled me away. They handcuffed the young man and we all drove back to the school in their squad car.

Again, I wondered what was happening to me – and why?

The kids and many colleagues warned me not to press charges, saying the gang would seek retribution and kill me. Even the police said that it could mean serious trouble, but it was important that I take a stand. I filed charges.

Several weeks later, I was ordered to appear in court to testify. Our school security officer and several off-duty LAPD officers, all new friends of mine, accompanied me. As we walked down the hall to the courtroom, the gang lined both sides of the hall and flashed me threatening looks. I was never so relieved to have friends who carried guns; my non-violent beliefs were really being tested! The young man who hit me was dressed in a shirt and tie, and looked much different, less menacing. After hearing the testimony and considering the evidence, the judge found the young man guilty and locked him up.

Word on the street was that I had a contract on my head. I received occasional threats, but my colleagues and kids learned that one can stand up to violence. To this day, I don't know if I would have made the same decision if I had actually lived in one of these gang-controlled neighborhoods. What became clear is that the kids in the school saw me in a new light and showed me a heightened respect.

That same semester, I began to work the playground after school. Now living on my own, I needed the extra money to pay rent. I got to know Mr. Walton, the gray-haired black man who had joked with me that first morning in the teachers' cafeteria. He continued my informal education, helping me to understand the lives of my kids and the context in which they were living. I'll never forget one of our conversations late one afternoon as we were locking up the gym and putting the equipment away. I asked, "Mr. Walton, Why do we always have to wear ties in this school? It's filthy and hot and the tie just gets in the way."

He responded in a very still and deep voice, "Because it's a sign of respect to these kids and their community."

I'll never forget his message: respect flows in two directions and is transmitted in many subtle ways. Another piece of the foundation of what would become *Sacred Leadership* fell into place. His wisdom informs me to this day, even though I haven't seen him for over 30 years.

While supervising the playground, I developed relationships with kids who weren't in my classroom or part of my science club; I began to connect with them in new ways. They were surprised that a white man like me could play basketball, and intrigued to hear stories about my upbringing. They were shocked to learn that my grandparents had no running water or indoor plumbing, that they had not completed school beyond the third grade, and that my parents were the first in their immediate families to finish high school. In many ways, they learned that we weren't all that different. By the end of the year, rumor had it I was really black!

At the close of the year, I was honored with the "Rookie Teacher of the Year" award by the administration and faculty. Of all the awards I have received from city and state governments, professional associations and businesses, I cherish this one the most, because it was awarded by my peers for doing one of the most important jobs in the world.

• • • • •

Following this very exciting and challenging first year of my career, I served 19 years in the inner city schools of Los Angeles, filling positions from teacher to high school principal. Those were years of great learning and were both personally and professionally fulfilling.

In 1989, I moved to a suburban school district in La Cañada, California, where I served eight years as a school leader – the last five as superintendent.

For the last fifteen years, I have been involved in leadership development and executive coaching in schools, non-profits and entrepreneurial businesses. I have found the issues to be similar, regardless of the setting. Everyone with whom I work is struggling to understand and operate in this rapidly changing environment while also trying to find meaning and purpose in their lives and work.

During my career I have had the opportunity to observe a few outstanding leaders, many good managers – and one or two people who should never have been put in charge. Each taught me in some way; for that I am grateful. From most I learned a great deal about what to do. From the others, I learned what not to do.

However, my first year of teaching is where my journey of *Sacred Leadership* began. It was then that I connected to a mission and purpose so strong that I kept my word, which I shared that first day of school: "Good morning, I am Mr. Davis and I am going to be your teacher for the rest of the year…I'm different – now let's get on with the lesson."

Little did I know those young people also had lessons for me. At the age of 22, I am not sure I consciously grasped these and other lessons that first year. However, they certainly began to influence me and my development as a leader. The lessons included:
- Stay connected to a purpose that serves something greater than yourself.
- Though difficult, always follow your values – it is essential.
- No one can do it alone. We need others to be successful.
- Community and relationships are crucial.
- Enlist others in solving problems.

- Stop judging and start listening in order to see more clearly.
- Show respect and a little empathy.
- Don't give up.
- Be courageous.

Each of these lessons helped shape my perspective and understanding of the world, underscored my belief that I could influence that world, shaped the principles outlined in this book and formed the foundation of *Sacred Leadership*.

Chapter 2 Questions for Reflection

1. What is your story?

2. Do you "own" your story – both the good and the bad?

3. What are the major lessons to be learned from your story?

4. How has your story influenced your leadership practice?

"We are explorers and the most compelling frontier of our time is human consciousness. Our quest is the integration of science and spirituality, a vision which reminds us of our connectedness to the inner self, to each other, and to the earth." [16]

—Edgar Mitchell, Apollo Astronaut

Chapter 3

GREATEST GOOD

The First Principle of *Sacred Leadership*

Four principles form the foundation of *Sacred Leadership*. The first principle is serving the greatest good. This principle describes the "what" and "why" of leadership in an organization. It speaks to purpose and serving something greater than ourselves.

However, within this first principle, a critical distinction – between the common good and the greatest good – did not become clear to me until my beliefs were challenged early in my professional career.

A Challenge to Beliefs

In the late 1970s, at age 29, I was thrown into the heat of the court-ordered desegregation being implemented in the Los Angeles Unified School District. A faction of the school board was opposed to the desegregation plan and it seemed they were withholding resources in an effort to hinder implementation. The superintendent assigned me to open and coordinate a magnet school for gifted middle school students. The school was located in central Los Angeles. As the beginning of the school year approached, chaos and emotion across the city increased. Despite the political turmoil within the school board, my team and I did everything within our power to insure a safe and positive start to the school year.

The Los Angeles Unified School District covers nearly 500 square miles and I had students being bused from nearly every corner of the city. My bus supervisor's office was a yellow school bus. He must have lived in this "office on wheels" during those first few weeks of the year – at least I thought so. In his bus he had a large map of the district on a piece of cardboard and used push pins to highlight the location of each of my 500 assigned students (that's what I mean by a lack of resources!) and the routes each of our fifteen buses would follow. The day before school was to open the majority of my students had not received notification of their bus pick-up points from the school district headquarters. We worked late into the evening, personally calling to inform students about the location of their bus stops and their estimated pick-up times.

The next morning, I was at work by 5:00 a.m. to monitor the news channels and coordinate with police who patrolled the perimeter of our school. There were protests at many schools, and a few protestors, mostly mothers of young children, chained themselves to some of the buses. Along with our custodial staff, we had completed a deep sweep of our campus to insure there were no bombs or other hazards planted overnight. In addition, threats had been made to shoot at the school buses as they traversed the freeways. Each of the buses had a unique identification number painted on the roof. Helicopters patrolled the sky, providing a sense of security in a war-like atmosphere as tens of thousands of kids began their year in new schools all across the district.

As the buses rolled up in front of my school, the kids were greeted and escorted to their new classrooms. The staff was primed to make everyone feel at home. As the last bus arrived and the final group of students found their way to class, I breathed a huge sigh of relief, believing that I was doing my part to serve the "common good." Decades of segregation and inferior education for poor and minority kids were coming to a welcome end in Los Angeles.

...or so I thought.

More than 30 years later, the Los Angeles Unified School District is more segregated than ever. Student achievement is lower and dropout rates higher. Meanwhile, Los Angeles has been rocked by race riots, and relationships between different ethnic groups remain intense and often explosive. What happened to that "common good" in which I so fervently believed?

Some of my most basic beliefs and assumptions were challenged through this experience and many others like it, forcing me to re-think my conception of the common good.

The Common Good

Generally, *common good* describes a specific benefit that is shared by all (or most) members of a given community. From my perspective, the common good is "local" in nature, serving a specific community or even a group within a community. Public schools, hospitals, fire and police departments all represent a local community's agreement on the common good of education, health care, and safety. We also experience efforts to serve the common good in our personal lives. Some examples include our work as volunteers, blood donors or our efforts to provide support for our local non-profit organizations.

Historical Perspective

The discussion of the common good goes back to the time of Aristotle, who said "…one citizen differs from another, but the salvation of the community is the common business of them all."[17] Aristotle strongly argued that democracy was the best form of government to serve the common good; however, those in power narrowly defined those to be included. This outlook has survived for centuries; among other ignominious pieces of our history, it allowed the reality of slavery to live alongside the ideal of democracy.

And so it is today. The language of the 2008 presidential campaigns reflected this. Candidates Obama and McCain both referred to the common good but often with very different meanings. Why? Because for each candidate, who belonged under the tent called the "commons" was different. It seems that not much has changed since Aristotle's time!

The idea of the commons in America dates back to the open-field practice in England. Around each English manor were "open-fields," where villagers grew crops and raised livestock for their own use. This practice was brought to America in the form of commons in New England cities, towns and villages. The Boston Commons is probably the best known to Americans. When Boston was created in 1635, pastureland was set aside for the grazing of livestock. Individuals were responsible not to overgraze the Commons to the detriment of others. As their animals grazed, neighbors gathered and conversed, building a sense of community. While in Boston recently I walked through this famous site. Though now surrounded by one of America's more compact and congested cities, the Boston Commons continues to provide an open space where the human soul of the city's populace can come and be rejuvenated.

Inherent Conflict

Our nation has a split personality, in which our heritage of strong individualism often conflicts with our belief in the common good. We see this dichotomy in our founding documents. The Declaration of Independence reads:

> *We hold these Truths to be self-evident, that all Men are created equal, that they are endowed by their Creator with certain inalienable Rights, that among these are Life, Liberty and the Pursuit of Happiness – That to secure these Rights, Governments are instituted among Men, deriving their just Powers from the Consent of the Governed…* [18]

Here, it is clear that our Founders were focused on the individual rights of citizens. It states that government was formed not for their common good, but rather to insure each individual's rights to "Life, Liberty and the Pursuit of Happiness."

Contrast this with our other great founding document, The United States Constitution, which seems to focus more on the common good and the general welfare of the people when it says:

> *We the People of the United States, in Order to form a more perfect Union, establish Justice, insure domestic Tranquility, provide for the common defense, promote the general Welfare, and secure the Blessings of Liberty to ourselves and Posterity, do ordain and establish this Constitution for the United States of America.*[19]

The conflict between strong individualism and our sense of community has remained with us since our founding. At first glance, it seems that it should be easy to reach agreement on what we call the common good. However, this conflict between individual and community needs often becomes a point of contention that leaders must deal with. Leaders may assume there is agreement when defining the common good, but in practice it is often not the case. Even when there is agreement on the ends (i.e. education, health care, safety), the means to achieve them are often hot topics in local politics.

The two stories that follow illustrate this dichotomy.

As the Times Square Ball in New York dropped to herald the arrival of 2011, California entered its ninth year of drought. Today in my home city, there is debate over water rationing. Although few argue about the need to conserve this precious resource, the conversation has been difficult and contentious. City leaders feel that more development is vitally important to the economic well-being (common good) of the community. However, out-of-control development has increased water usage citywide and led to the need for residential rationing. Local residents feel this does not serve the common good nor does it recognize their individual rights because lawns and gardens are now dying from lack of water, leading to decreased property values, increased fire danger and a diminished quality of life. The missing link is a discussion about the kind of community we want and how we, as a community, will define the common good and the individual rights of our citizens.

A similar scenario materialized when a family friend bought an old farm in Indiana. He refurbished the barn and converted it into a comfortable home for his family. A small, serene lake on the property was stocked with fish and provided hours of pleasant relaxation for his family and friends.

Years later, a large commercial hog operation relocated next to his small farm. Soon, thousands of pigs had generated tons of smelly waste, the stench of which blew downwind to his home. One of the holding ponds for the waste ruptured, its foul contents flowing into and ruining his lake. Legal battles ensued.

What was the common good in this case? Was the common good defined by his family's needs? Or the need of the commercial pork company to produce meat for the marketplace? Or, perhaps, the need of the consumer for low-cost pork? These are complex issues. Some say that the common good is defined as the individual's basic right to freely shape his or her life by responsible action that does not infringe upon another's same right. Under this definition, our family friend probably comes out on top.

Still others try to resolve the issue by defining the common good as the greatest possible good for the greatest number of individuals. In that case, my friend certainly loses on a daily basis, as millions sit down to dinner with barbecued pork ribs! But somehow, that doesn't feel right because the hog owner exercised his individual rights by infringing on the rights of his neighbor.

In both examples, it became clear to me that these definitions took us down the proverbial rabbit hole in Alice's Wonderland. It seemed that neither definition really addressed or clarified the common good in a way that was fair for either party.

The Conflict Continues

Today, the debate continues to play out locally and nationally with some believing strongly that individuals and corporations, with few exceptions, should only answer to the free market economy. Contrast this with others who hold an equally passionate desire for government intervention to end poverty, to provide health care and security or even to manage the economy. The former camp is now labeled "conservative Republicans" and the latter "liberal Democrats."

Our current political leaders do not seem to comprehend or appreciate the inherent contradiction between individualism and the common good. As the debates by academics and politicians continue, so does the inherent conflict.

However, the majority of Americans are very clear about where they stand. A 2006 study by the Center for American Progress found that 85% of voters *agreed* (68% **strongly agreed**) that the *government should be committed to the common good and put the public's interest above the privileges of the few.*[20]

Contrast this with the political debate following Hurricane Irene (August 2011) in which some insisted that it is the individual's responsibility (or at least the state's responsibility) to provide for disaster relief and questioned increased funding for the Federal Emergency Management Agency (FEMA).

Neither side seems to understand that many people can, and do, build lives and organizations that utilize both precepts. In the hardened views of these camps, you're either one or the other. The failure of our leaders to recognize and address this dichotomy has led to in-civility and gridlock in the work of our public institutions.

What is required today is leadership that not only understands this dichotomy, but that can also articulate it; leadership that can engage the populace in a dialogue that recognizes and honors both perspectives. Rather than labeling others as bad, wrong or stupid, we must understand that these are two different worldviews that can and must be reconciled. This may sound like we are asking for toasted ice, but I believe it is not only possible, it is absolutely necessary.

From the Common Good to the Greatest Good

In spite of these inherent conflicts, the common good worked relatively well when we lived in small, isolated, tribal communities. However, the world has globalized and our numbers and technology have advanced to the point that we have disrupted our own ecology. Our ability to understand our interconnectedness has been strained. What appears to be the common good for one community or group today often represents disaster, illness or environmental degradation for another. We are no longer separate or isolated.

I spoke of my struggle with the idea of the common good to a colleague I was visiting in Arizona. She asked, "Why would you focus on 'common' good? Why not the 'greater' good, or better yet, the 'greatest' good?" I was dumbstruck! I went for a quiet walk in the desert and realized that she was absolutely right. My concerns as a leader transcend my local community or even my country. The world is far too interconnected to ignore the impact of our actions at the global level. The semantic difference between the "common good" and "greatest good" reveals a much larger perspective that must be considered, one that incorporates the entire planet.

I realized that my true interest as a human being lies with this marvelous planet we call home – all of its inhabitants, all of its creation. As leaders we honor our immediate responsibility to serve what is sacred in our own organizations and communities. However, we also understand that neither we nor our organizations operate in isolation, but rather in connection with all others on this planet. Since we are connected, we influence and are influenced by this global environment and all it encompasses.

Consciousness and Connectedness

We have a choice to either lead from consciousness of our interconnectedness and interdependence – or, if not, to lead from ignorance and unconsciousness. This consciousness is more than a physical sensing of what is around us; it is a deep-felt understanding of our connectedness that goes beyond simple awareness. The way of consciousness may seem (and often is) more difficult, but it is only through conscious leadership that we can achieve the sacred purpose of serving the greatest good. Any other approach is simply too limited and by its limitations contributes to the problems of the world. Unconsciousness leads to the reliving of the past rather than living into the surprising possibilities that emerge in our daily lives. As leaders we must not only serve our missions, but do so in a manner that recognizes our connectedness on a global scale and honors our spiritual well-being, our fellow human beings, our greater environment and all it contains.

There is, in fact, a greatest good and we need not fear appearing naïve when we speak of it. Mahatma Gandhi, Nelson Mandela and Mother Theresa are all examples of those who have followed this path. We look at them as amazing examples but each of us, in our leadership practice and in our daily lives, can embrace our missions of serving the greatest good – the first principle of *Sacred Leadership.*

When leaders maintain consciousness of our global interconnectedness and the greatest good, they are able to raise that consciousness in those with whom they live, work and interact. Leaders, while serving the sacred missions of their own organizations, realize that, through their own example, they are helping others become conscious and reconnect to the greatest good.

Movement – from Old to New

We now have a better understanding of how our interconnectedness and interdependence moves us from the common good to the greatest good. But the question remains, how do we begin to move those we lead from the old paradigm to the new?

Researchers at the MIT Sloan School of Management suggest that, "The primary problem with the present era is that we're between stories. The old story that bound Western culture, the story of reductionist science and redemptive religion is breaking down. It simply no longer explains the world we are experiencing or the changes that confront us...Outside the core we don't yet have a new story that's clear enough, simple enough and widely understood enough to serve a new community of thought."[21]

A key role of the leader is to help the community see and embrace the new era. He or she uses hindsight to gain an understanding of the past and develop insight into the past's relationship with the present. Most importantly, the leader helps the community develop foresight so it may begin to write the new story that wants or needs to emerge. This story is a positive experience that reflects a commitment to the greatest good. The MIT researchers maintain that, "The most important thing going forward is to break the boundaries between people so we can operate as a single intelligence."[22]

We need to see boundaries not as walls that separate us, but as opportunities for connection and understanding. This requires suspending judgment and listening deeply to others with different perspectives.

Dee Hock, the founder of Visa, noted, "It is essential to determine with absolute clarity, shared understanding and deep conviction the *Purpose* of the community. From that, all else must flow...Purpose is a clear simple statement of intent that identifies and binds the community together as a worthy pursuit. It is an unambiguous expression of that which people jointly wish to become."[23]

He goes on to say "Purpose and principle...cannot be devised by leaders and imposed on a community as a condition of participation. They must be evoked from the minds and hearts of members of the community."[24]

What might this new paradigm look like? How does *Sacred Leadership*, help "evoke" this purpose "from the hearts and minds" of those in your community or organization?

Using the story about desegregation in Los Angeles that began this chapter, the following text boxes first provide a lens for looking at the old paradigm and then a view through the lens of *Sacred Leadership* and the greatest good.

Old Paradigm – A Management Approach

The old paradigm takes a management and problem solving approach that looks something like this:

Identify the Problem

They asked: "How can we overcome the negative consequences of segregation in our schools?" The assumptions were that segregated schools led to poor education, increased racial tensions, etc. Few questioned the underlying causes of segregation or the assumptions they were making about its impact on educational achievement.

Identify the Solution

Desegregation was based upon old paradigms, old ways of thinking and limited understanding. The solution became narrowly focused on a combination of means, forced and voluntary busing and the redistribution of resources. An example would be taking money from instructional programs and using it for transportation, additional security etc. Success was primarily framed in terms of the number of kids transported and the ethnic make-up of the newly comprised schools (designed to reflect the ethnic make-up of Los Angeles).

The Outcomes

- Schools were integrated for a short time.
- Some students received improved education.
- Some students received inferior education.
- "White flight" led to re-segregation.
- Connections between local communities and their schools were lost.
- Many stereotypes were reinforced.
- The quality of education deteriorated.
- Dropout rates increased.
- Racial tensions increased.

If the leaders in Los Angeles had asked questions about what the community wanted and needed, rather than acting on untested assumptions, they could have developed different actions that would have led to different outcomes.

New Paradigm –
A *Sacred Leadership* Approach

Because "Sacred Leadership" focuses on serving the greatest good, it begins by bringing people together and asking questions, thus clarifying and gaining commitment to the mission. First and foremost, it is about realizing possibilities inherent in the mission, rather than solving problems. We must change our mindset and move away from problem solving and into possibility thinking.

Identify the Possibilities

The leaders ask questions like: "What do we want for the children of our city? What needs to emerge that serves the best interests of our children, our families, our communities and our country? What do our children need to be successful global citizens?" They move the discussion from individual, to local, to a more global perspective.

Through the years I have led many community groups in these discussions about the hopes, dreams and aspirations they have for their children. I have found the World Café[25] serves as a useful model for structuring these conversations. It provides an easily organized process for engaging hundreds, or even thousands, of people in dialogue. My experience is that, when asking questions like those above, communities usually articulate possibilities like:

- *We want our kids to be happy.*
- *We want our kids to be healthy and safe.*
- *We want our kids to have an excellent education that*

will provide them choices upon graduation.

- We want our kids to be prepared for the jobs of the future.
- We want our kids to be prepared for the global society of the future

Note that these possibilities leave little room for argument. The focus is on the greatest good for these children, not on our differences of opinion. The possibilities are also more expansive and go beyond the classroom, school or community. They begin to define a greater purpose of educating and nurturing our children. The energy of the group now flows into realizing these possibilities rather than fomenting disagreement over minor issues.

Take Action

- Prototype several of the possibilities. Avoid wholesale organizational change at the beginning.
- Measure incremental results and adjust.
- Institutionalize those prototypes that work.

Outcomes

- The conversation typically moves beyond the schoolhouse door to recognize that the entire community must be involved in order to realize the dreams and aspirations of our children.
- Typically, health care providers, law enforcement, the juvenile justice system, social services and local, state and federal government resources are brought to bear

in realizing such an emerging dream.

- *Resources begin to appear as others connect with the dream.*

Finally, we measure outcomes, adjust and dream some more! The process continues; we have fun and enjoy the journey together.

Getting Unstuck

Having looked in more detail at these two different approaches, we see that they get very different results. So how do we move from the old management paradigm to the new paradigm of serving the greatest good? To initiate this movement from old to new is one of the most difficult points in the change process. We often feel mired in the muck of the old paradigm that keeps us stuck in the old ways of doing things. The important thing is to focus on building forward momentum rather than focusing on being stuck.

In the practice of *Sacred Leadership*, leaders diligently work in a proactive manner rather than reverting to old patterns of the past. They begin by: 1) convening the right people, 2) asking the right questions to elicit the possibilities inherent in the situation and 3) unveiling and recognizing the obstacles and beliefs that block agreement. Let's look at each of these actions in more detail.

1. Getting Unstuck: Convening the Right People

Leaders convene the right people; those that have the knowledge, skills, desire and influence to move the process forward in the early stages.

They are not so naïve as to believe that they can hold a meeting and come to agreement about serving the greatest good. Nor can they expect their constituents and stakeholders to easily move from the old paradigm to the new. Changing our focus from personal and local needs to group and global needs is not easy. Our natural survival instincts – to take care of ourselves and our tribe – constantly compete with our desire to serve something greater. It is very similar to the dichotomy I described earlier in this chapter – balancing our deeply felt desire for individual rights with the need to serve the general welfare.

We will explore enlisting and engaging others in more detail in Chapter 5 when we discuss the third principle of *Sacred Leadership*.

2. Getting Unstuck: Identifying Possibilities

Next leaders ask questions that elicit the possibilities inherent in the situation. In Chapter 6 we will discuss the use of foresight, the fourth principle of *Sacred Leadership*, to help uncover these possibilities.

3. Getting Unstuck: Unveiling and Recognizing Obstacles

Finally, leaders unveil and recognize the obstacles and beliefs that block agreement. The goal is not to focus on the obstacles, but rather to understand them so they do not get in our way. Focusing on obstacles is the old paradigm of problem solving. Rather than trying to eliminate obstacles, we focus our time, energy and resources helping the desired possibility emerge.

The work of Velasquez and Andre outlined in the following text boxes provides a framework for understanding the obstacles that often appear.

A Framework for Understanding Obstacles to the Common Good

Writing in the journal "Ethics," Manuel Velasquez and Claire Andre identified four obstacles that hinder us as a society from shifting from the old, locally centered, paradigm to the new paradigm of serving the greatest good.[26] Their language is couched in the terminology of the common good but it easily translates to my conception of the greatest good.

Obstacle One – Our Differences

According to Velasquez and Andre, the first obstacle is that "the very idea of the common good is inconsistent with a pluralistic society."[27] Those who take such a position say that, as a people, we are too different to agree upon what constitutes the good life for each of our citizens.

While we certainly encounter this obstacle, it does not need to deter our forward momentum. Differences only get in the way if we choose to focus on them. From a biological and evolutionary perspective, cooperation is in our DNA. We know that cooperation is a necessary foundation for survival and success. We learn to negotiate our differences and work out cooperative schemes for our mutual benefit.[28] While taking care of their individual needs, living things must also ensure the survival of the entire system on which they are dependent. Leaders need to build this type of awareness into their organizations. To do this, leaders relentlessly focus on the greatest good they are trying to achieve rather than on the differences. Inherently, we possess more similarities with each other than differences.

Obstacle Two – "Free-Riders"

The second obstacle is referred to as the "free-rider" problem. "The benefits that a common good provides are...available to everyone, including those who choose not to do their part to maintain the common good."[29] These free-riders cause some to hesitate to spend their time and resources when others refuse to do their part.

In my experience, it is rare for an individual to not connect with his or her true purpose in life once it has been discovered. In organizations, I believe the free-rider obstacle is more an issue of the person being on the "wrong bus." Because free-riders haven't connected with the mission with both their heart and mind, they are often not willing to commit to the larger purpose. In a community that is based upon "sacred" purpose, there is a self-regulating system that makes it difficult for the free-rider to exist. Leaders and their community members don't allow free-riders to remain, because they take precious resources away from their sacred purpose. They first approach the free-rider with an open mind and heart and good will to support everyone's participation in their efforts. That failing, the free-rider is asked (sometimes forced) to "get off the bus" and find a new place that embodies a sacred mission that speaks to him or her.

Obstacle Three – Individualism

Velasquez and Andre write that the "… third problem encountered by attempts to promote the common good is that of individualism."[30] Healthy communities are built upon two pillars of equal strength and necessity: a commitment to the common good and a respect for the freedoms of individuals. Renowned Professor Amitai Etzioni commented in his blog that "In order for our society to continue and to flourish, all of its members must work toward this balance between rights and responsibility…"[31] The leader's role is to help people understand these two competing ideas and guide them toward the balance of rights and responsibilities.

The leader incorporates these two perspectives into the organization's stories and articulates the inherent conflict as the organization attempts to balance this dichotomy in its day-to-day decision-making.

Obstacle Four – Unequal Sharing of the Burden

Finally, Velasquez and Andre write, "Appeals to the common good are confronted by the problem of an unequal sharing of the burdens. Maintaining a common good often requires that particular individuals or particular groups bear costs that are much greater than those borne by others."[32]

This obstacle is based on a model of scarcity, which contrasts with "Sacred Leadership" – a model of abundance. *As we move to possibilities based on the greatest good, more resources appear, people become more committed and the burden is spread more fairly. As we change our seeing from a problem-solving mode to a possibilities mode, we are able to identify resources previously hidden from us. In addition, by their very nature, possibilities attract resources, whereas problems consume them. We are not splitting the same proverbial pie among more people, but rather we a creating a growing pie.*

When practicing "Sacred Leadership," leaders are aware of each of these obstacles and see them as realities that must be "understood" rather than problems that must be solved. As they focus on emerging possibilities, obstacles tend to dissolve of their own accord because people are deeply committed to serving the greatest good.

In the last text box, I took time to discuss the obstacles that can confront us, but remember that is just the third of three actions for getting unstuck as the leader moves away from problem-solving toward possibility and the greatest good. To recap, those actions are:

1. convening the right people,
2. asking the right questions to elicit the possibilities inherent in the situation and
3. unveiling and recognizing the obstacles and beliefs that block agreement.

Fortunately, the vast majority of our society reports a willingness to give in order to receive. Most of us seem willing to balance our commitment to strong individualism with the collective needs of our society to fulfill the common good. With increased understanding of our global interconnectedness, we will be even more amenable to balancing our individualism to fulfill the "greatest good."

The Challenge

Professor of Philosophy, Kwame Anthony Appiah describes the challenge of the greatest good very succinctly. "The challenge is to take minds and hearts formed over long millennia of living in local troops and equip them with ideas and institutions that allow us to live together as the *global* tribe we have become."[33]

So often, many leaders focus on our differences rather than our similarities, making it nearly impossible to come to agreement on the greatest good. This has been especially true in the political arena. As we practice *Sacred Leadership* we can use the tools and approaches shared in this chapter to help us recognize our areas of agreement and move into dialogue and beyond gridlock to action that identifies and serves the greatest good of "the global tribe we have become."

Chapter 3 Questions for Reflection

1. What is the sacred purpose of your organization? How does your sacred purpose or mission serve the greatest good?

2. Have you considered a truly global context in framing your connection to the greatest good?

3. How does your mission or sacred purpose impact this greatest good?
   a. Is the impact positive or negative?
   b. How do you know?

4. How well have you articulated this purpose and connected it to the greatest good? How could you communicate this more effectively?

5. How does the conflict between individual needs and the greatest good manifest in your organization? How do you address this conflict?

6. In the 'rat race' of daily life, how do you maintain consciousness of the larger whole of which you are a part?

7. How do you support those you lead in maintaining this larger perspective?

8. What are the different influences, within and outside your organization, that make it difficult to agree on the greatest good you are serving? How are you reconciling these differences?

9. Who are the "free-riders" within your organization? How can you motivate them to become meaningful participants and contributors in your work?

10. How can you recognize and accommodate the individual needs of people within your organization while ensuring that your sacred purpose and the greatest good are served?

11. How does the obstacle of unequal sharing reveal itself within your organization? How can you mitigate this issue?

*"This is a law-abiding universe.
This is a moral universe.
It hinges on moral foundations.
If we are to make of this a better
world, we've got to go back
and rediscover that precious
value that we've left behind"* [34]
—*Martin Luther King Jr.*

Chapter 4

SHARED AND ENDURING VALUES

The Second Principle of *Sacred Leadership*

Shared and enduring values form the basis of the second principle of *Sacred Leadership*. Whereas the first principle spoke to the "what" and "why" of leadership, the second principle speaks to the "how," the means by which we achieve our ends. Shared values describe how we serve our mission and interact with our clients and those within our organization. I am not referring to some technique, process or methodology. Rather I am asking how we use our higher principles and values to guide our individual and collective behaviors and actions.

Values are fundamental principles that describe standards of behavior, especially in our relationship to others. Honesty, mutual respect, compassion and integrity are representative of the kind of values that are so deeply held that they are called core values. Beyond their implicit meaning, we can ascribe specific behaviors to each of these values. For instance, integrity could be defined as "doing what you say you are going to do, even when no one is watching." Mutual respect might be described as "treating others as you wish to be treated." What is important here is the fact that individuals and teams can describe or operationalize their values in positive behavioral terms.[35]

Often when I work with groups, they identify money, free time, making a profit or having fun as values. From a *Sacred Leadership* perspective, these are not core values; they are simply products or things that we value or desire. They merely represent an outcome of our behavior, whereas core values define how, in behavioral terms, we will achieve those outcomes.

The "Not So Soft" Side of Leadership

In the late 1990s, I was struggling to understand the discrepancy in student achievement between the inner city kids I had worked with and those I had served in the suburbs. I had come to the conclusion that the lower student achievement in the inner city was primarily related to the chaotic nature of the environment in which these kids lived. One day, I was sharing this idea with a friend, who was a college president. He said, "Jim, if you want to know about leading in chaotic environments, you should talk to the people at the United States Army War College." He gave me the contact. Although I wasn't quite sure what I would learn, I called Colonel Jeffrey McCausland, who served as Dean of Academics, United States Army War College – the Army's graduate school where their strategic leaders are trained and developed.

When Colonel McCausland answered the telephone, I explained why I was calling and gave him a brief overview of my background. He said, "Look, this is the Army *War* College – I don't know anything about K-12 education."

"Well," I said, "Do you know anything about leading in chaos?"

He responded, "Of course, that's easy – Values, Mission, and Goals!"

The last word I expected to hear at the top of his list was "values," Colonel McCausland articulated those values as we spoke: Loyalty, Duty, Respect, Selfless Service, Honor, Integrity and Personal Courage.

My telephone call to Colonel McCausland led to an opportunity to visit the Army War College in Carlisle, PA and meet with several faculty members. In our discussions, it became clear that values were not seen as the "soft side" of leadership. To the Army, the application of clear, well-defined and deeply held values is *fundamental* to leading in the chaos of battle as well as leading day-to-day. These weren't just words to the servicemen and women I met; these values were deeply felt and held guideposts for their behavior and actions.

Several months later, I was invited to participate in a National Security Seminar. Once there, I was assigned to one of the War College seminar groups. I found, to a person, that these individuals could not only name these values, but also define them in behavioral terms. They could describe what these values were and were not and, most importantly, they demonstrated the values through their actions during the week I was with them.

These Army leaders understood that "values give an organization a self-ordering quality, a kind of organizational ballast, which provides direction and stability in periods of turmoil, stress and change...Effective leaders understand that core values rooted deeply within people who make up an organization are the essence of its organizational culture and an enormous source of strength."[36]

In contrast, values rarely came up as I discussed these same leadership issues with my university and school district colleagues or with my clients from the business, corporate, non-profit and public sectors. Values were never discussed in my university classes as I completed my Master's Degree and doctoral work. Only once was the issue of values raised as I worked with several Fortune 500 CEOs. Few of my educator colleagues ever discussed values in the context of their work.

This missing emphasis on values convinced me that a large part of the discrepancy in student achievement I was trying to understand, and what led me to the Army War College, might be the result not only of the chaotic environment inner city kids faced but also the product of a values system gone awry.

Far from being the "soft side" of leadership, the story below describes how powerfully values influence the outcomes of our work.

Values Do Affect Outcomes

In 2002, I was asked to lead a five-year leadership development program in a K-12 school district. The goal of the program was to build a pipeline of future leaders within the district. Our focus was on developing the whole leader – what is called the "Be, Know, Do" of leadership.[37]

At our first offsite retreat, we took the group through a values exercise. First, we asked them to identify the values they held most dear as individuals. Next, they were asked to form a consensus on the values that would guide their group as they worked together over the next 18 months. They came up with a list of five: honesty, caring, respect, integrity and loyalty and then described each in behavioral terms. As a mental exercise about values it was very engaging, but for most of the group, I felt the learning just stopped there.

After a short break, the group reassembled in our meeting room. There was a lot of positive energy and conversation; things were going well. However, I perceived a disconnection between the values activity and the participants' understanding of its application to their roles as leaders. I decided to move our agenda in a slightly different direction.

I distributed a set of data showing student achievement in an unnamed school district with an ethnically diverse student population that was predominantly Hispanic but also included sizable populations of Black, White and Asian students. Many of the students were also identified as English language learners. Most of the families could be called working poor. The data included test scores, graduation rates, college preparation rates, etc. It also went deeper, framing the data in subsets by gender, ethnicity, English learner and socio-economic status (SES). I asked them to look at the data, discuss their impressions and be prepared to share their observations with the entire group.

After some animated discussions, members of the group reported that they were appalled by the disparity in achievement between Hispanic and Black students compared to their Caucasian and Asian counterparts. It was also clear that the English learner students were at a disadvantage, as were students of low SES. They asked, "How could a school district allow this to happen?"

"Well, what values are reflected in this data?" I asked.

My question was met with puzzled looks, but soon the discussion took off. "Certainly these educators were uncaring and probably a bit racist," one responded. "No one is paying attention to these kids!" said another. Someone else commented, "Is there no respect for these kids and their families, and where is the professional integrity of this staff?" The discussion went on in this vein for several minutes.

Finally, someone asked the question I'd been waiting for: "What school district is this?"

I looked the person straight in the eye and said, "Yours."

My comment was met with disbelief, then denial, followed by excuses and finally tears. I then rephrased the question, "How are *your* values reflected in this data?"

The group was now very emotional. After spending so much time identifying their core values, they could not reconcile their student achievement results with the values they espoused.

It happened; this was the breakthrough I was after! The conversations took on a new and much deeper meaning. Their focus seemed more closely aligned to the broader purpose of educating and nurturing their students. The group began to look at the discrepancy in student achievement with new eyes. They explored the organizational values that seemed to be reflected in the data. They realized that sometimes leaders are unaware of deeply hidden values, and in this case, beliefs that are influencing their work. Of course many variables affect student achievement, but *Sacred Leadership* recognizes that underlying values are fundamental. All of the new curriculum, instructional processes and structures will not make a difference if the underlying values and beliefs do not support the idea that all students can and should achieve at high levels. The group now understood that, in fact, values affect outcomes.

The Role of Values in Organizations

So how do our values affect the success of the organizations we lead? It is as important to describe how we are to achieve our goals as it is to describe those goals. The clear identification and articulation of values is crucial in the execution of decisions, because values serve many purposes in organizations. Values serve as a *moral compass* to guide decisions and action; as a *foundation* that provides stability during growth and chaos; as a *magnet* that attracts people with like values and as *glue* that holds members of a team together, especially in difficult times; as an *identity* that defines the team; and as a *measuring device* that sets standards for both individual and team performance.[38] Let's look at each of these in more detail.

Values as Moral Compass

First and foremost, enduring personal and organizational values provide boundaries within which we act. Values such as integrity, respect and compassion are signposts that define the parameters of our behavior. Commitment to shared values and communication of these values throughout the entire organization signal what we stand for and to what standards we are held accountable.

These parameters become even more important as the leadership environment becomes increasingly chaotic — what the Army calls

VUCA (Volatile, Uncertain, Complex and Ambiguous). In the heat of the moment, values serve as an internal moral compass that leaders may consult prior to making decisions or taking action. The leader asks, "Is the action I am about to take consistent with and in alignment with my core values and those of my organization?" Horrible and destructive decisions can often be avoided by taking a second to consult your moral compass before taking action.

In my consulting, I have found very little focus on values other than lip service. Unfortunately, company values posted on the wall, letterhead and website, often serve only as window dressing. When there is no connection between stated values and observed behaviors, the moral compass is lost.

As leaders, we are charged with making sure that values and behaviors are aligned. For example, during the recent recession, one of my clients was forced to lay off seventy employees. It was a very difficult task. The owners of the company first asked their senior managers to develop a potential layoff list. I advised the owners to look closely at the list and to retain the right to make final layoff decisions. When asked why, I explained, "It is difficult for senior managers to lay off those with whom they work closely and who are important contributors to their day-to-day performance. It is predictable that the majority of manager-recommended layoffs will be in positions far from the corporate office."

When the owners reviewed the layoff list, the prediction was verified and they were alarmed by the recommendations. It wasn't that the senior managers were bad or even wrong. From their perspective, they had worked diligently to make the best recommendations possible. At this point in the process, they were just blind to other possibilities.

Next, I asked the owners to review the layoff list in light of their mission and within the context of their stated organizational values.

Through this process, the list changed dramatically! They eliminated entire departments at the corporate level to spare positions that were at the working surfaces, where the employees most directly served their clients and the organization's mission.

Leaders, who practice *Sacred Leadership*, have a higher level of responsibility to protect the mission to serve the greatest good, and to align their decisions with their core values. Although all of the layoffs were painful, my client's final decision preserved the core mission, was consistent with the company's values and insured the financial viability of the company to the benefit of the remaining employees and the company's clients.

Values as a Foundation

By reflecting the individual human perspective, values provide a solid foundation for the organization through its leaders' actions. In their book *Hope is Not a Method*, Gordon Sullivan and Michael Harper write, "Shared values express the essence of an organization. They bind expectations; provide alignment and establish a foundation for transformation and growth. By emphasizing values, the leader signals what will not change, providing an anchor for people drifting in a sea of uncertainly and a strategic context for decision and actions that will grow the organization."[39]

Firmly held values, practiced on a day-to-day basis, provide a stability that can minimize the psychological trauma so often associated with rapid change. People are better able to predict actions and outcomes when the values are clear and articulated and the leaders honor those values in their daily interactions.

A set of values posted on the wall does nothing unless lived by the leadership. The values should signal how people will be treated, how decisions will be made and how consistency will be maintained in a changing world. Let's face it, the business environment is fluid and constantly changing; however, values are not.

Values as a Magnet and Glue

The values of an organization can serve as a magnet to other like-minded individuals. This does not mean we should build teams and organizations of people who all think alike. Diversity of opinion and perspective is important, even crucial, in developing innovative possibilities in our fast-paced environment.

Shared values insure that the way we act and behave toward one another and toward our customers and clients is consistent, predictable and respectful. They help us predict the behaviors of others and help us understand the underlying motivations behind those behaviors.

Shared values help us withhold judgment, enabling us to "see our seeing" and broaden our perspective on the range of emerging possibilities. Even if we don't like, agree with or understand a colleague's behavior or decision, we know, because of our shared values, that his/her intent originated from a positive place. Our shared values help us feel comfortable withholding judgment until things can be clarified, knowing our voice will be heard and our opinion and perspective honored. In this way shared positive values become glue that binds teams, organizations and communities together.

Patrick Lencioni, in his best-seller, *The Five Dysfunctions of a Team*, maintains that the absence of trust is the first dysfunction of ineffective teams.[40] Trust and mutual respect arise from shared values and bind team members together. They are absolutely critical to team and organizational effectiveness.

Values as an Identity

Shared values help define an organization and give it an identity. As individuals, we all have a desire to belong. Something deep within our DNA harkens back to our tribal past. Shared values, in concert with our mission to serve the greatest good, provide a connection with others in our organizations. Together they create an identity that connects us with one another, as well as signaling who we are collectively to the outside world.

Organizations that have a strong identity, built upon shared values and common purpose, engender greater commitment from their employees and customers. People take great pride in belonging to an organization that shares their values and feel a deeper connection to its purpose.

Values as a Measuring Device

Values also create a tool to measure individual, team and organizational performance. When our metrics measure our financial progress, efficient use of resources, customer and client feedback, etc., they are measuring crucial factors in gauging our progress toward achieving our goals. What we call *doing the right things*. However, it is equally important to measure the *doing things right* part of the equation.

Those who practice *Sacred Leadership* constantly reflect on the congruence between their values and their decisions, behaviors and actions. They also monitor the more subtle factor of doing things right *for the right reason*. The manner in which a leader treats the receptionist, custodian, an angry client or a colleague is monitored by employees, consciously or unconsciously, for consistency with the leader's stated values – believe me, the organization is watching and measuring!

A few years ago I met with the CEO of one of the largest insurers in California. When I arrived at the corporate headquarters, an older Hispanic man greeted us as we walked in the door. When I told him I was there to interview the CEO, he began telling me a story about how Tom (the CEO's first name) had helped him in a time of a family emergency. He said, "Tom always treats every employee, no matter their position, with respect." The enthusiasm he shared for the company was infectious! Yes, people are watching, and in this case the

CEO's behavior reflected the company's values in a very real way, gaining him the respect and commitment of his employees.

Periodically it is important to recalibrate the measuring device. Leaders should ask their employees, clients and other stakeholders to reflect on the organization's values. Also, organizations must consciously inculcate these values into their new employee induction programs. Leaders need to insure that the values are clear to the team and that they are incorporated into performance reviews. In fact, some experts suggest that up to 40% of a performance review should be based upon the employee's exhibiting the company values in their day-to-day work.[41] These formal processes raise organizational consciousness and increase values alignment and congruence throughout the company.

Developing Moral Authority

All leaders have positional authority. However, when operating from the higher purpose of serving the greatest good and in alignment with shared and enduring values, *Sacred Leadership* leads to a different kind of authority – moral authority. As they "walk their talk," leaders model moral authority throughout the organization. By example and expectation, they encourage others to operate from these same motivations – to serve the greatest good within the context of their shared values.

In organizations led by individuals who demonstrate moral authority, people do things right and do the right thing. They also do things for the right reasons – because they are in alignment with the mission and the values – not because their actions will earn praise, raises or promotions. This is sometimes the most difficult concept for managers to understand because they are operating from an old paradigm that depended upon extrinsic rewards for motivation. In coaching new managers, I stress first and foremost, that focusing on the organization's mission and acting in concert with its values will attract the best outcomes and greatest intrinsic rewards. The extrinsic rewards almost always follow without negatively influencing their behaviors or the outcomes.

Balancing Self-Interest

The issue of self-interest arises as leaders make decisions and move to action. In his book *Moral Leadership,* Thomas Sergiovanni argues that, "Our actions and our decisions are influenced by what we value and believe, as well as by self-interest. When the two are in conflict, values and beliefs usually take precedence."[42] Similarly, research conducted by Gallup, revealed that 91% of respondents agreed with the statement, "Duty comes before pleasure." Only 3% disagreed.[43] The results indicated that, when given the opportunity, the overwhelming majority of people would choose the common good of others over their narrow self-interests and they point to acts of altruism and heroism to support their perspective.

However, the above poll was conducted in 1988, and things may be changing. Newer research suggests that self-interest is becoming a more prevalent factor in our behavior. Numerous corporate examples referred to earlier in the book, showed that the behaviors of so many executives over the past decade and continuing today are based on self-interest, even to the point of greed. Most recently we were subjected to a new scandal involving the hacking of private telephones by employees of Rupert Murdoch's *News of the World* publication.[44] This revelation brought about widespread revulsion in Britain and the closure of the 163-year-old newspaper. It also caused a political scandal that reached into the government and the highly respected London police department. This latest example, tying self-interest to increased circulation and profits, supports the newer research that points out, "The impact of self-interest is pervasive. It can affect the decisions of the most thoughtful and upstanding leaders. It can influence our judgment even when we are trying to prevent it from doing so." The researchers added, "The evidence...suggests that decision makers are far more affected by self-interest than they claim and realize."[45]

The research goes on to report that a lack of awareness of the influence self-interest has on our decision making, "makes it particularly important to diagnose, because an unconscious influence is much harder for the decision maker to guard against."[46] We use self-awareness to constantly scan for consistency between our values and our actions. Through self-awareness I realized, in my first year of teaching, that my use of the paddle was inconsistent with my values. Even though corporal punishment seemed to be effective, I could no longer resort to its use.

In my consulting work, I have encountered conflict between my values and my financial self-interest. Early on, I realized that some of my clients were willing to pay for my services with no real intention of changing or following my advice. That often led to their failure and yet another crisis, which led to more consulting as I was often called in to help clean up the mess. My financial self-interest was served by staying with the client; however, my core values required in such cases that I "fire" them. I would not be living with integrity if I took their money knowing they had no real intention to grow and change.

Through self-awareness, leaders can bring their self-interest to consciousness. Now conscious of their self-interest, they use their values to short-circuit negative outcomes in favor of serving the greatest good. There are several questions leaders can ask themselves in an effort to identify the inappropriate influence of self-interest in their decision making.

Checking for the Inappropriate Influence
of Self-Interest

1. Does the decision I am about to make serve the mission of the organization and the greatest good?

2. Is the decision I am about to make consistent with my core values and those of the organization?

3. Knowing both the short- and long-term interests of my organization, are any of my choices particularly self-serving – am I making short-term decisions that suit my self-interest to the detriment of the long-term health of my company and its customers?

4. How might my self-interests significantly distort my decision?

5. Does the decision I am about to make recognize and provide for the future and take into account the second and third order consequences of my actions?

Self-interest is natural and can serve as a motivator for action. However, awareness of self- interest, especially in the context of our values, allows the leader to guard against and diminish its inappropriate influence in decision-making.

Congruence Between Personal and Organizational Values

Self-interest is not the only challenge to our practice of values-based leadership. Sometimes, the organizations in which we work are the problem. Leaders, when joining or leading a company, should look for alignment between their personal values and those of the organization. This does not mean that there is a 100% match of values, but it does require that most values are shared and not in conflict with each other. A large discrepancy between personal, team or organizational values decreases effectiveness and leads to increased levels of personal stress. When the discrepancy becomes too great, the leader must attempt to change the organization's values or leave.

It is critical that leaders develop acute awareness of and internalize their personal values. These must develop to a point where leaders are certain about the core values that govern their behavior. This is different from beliefs and ideas about the way the world works. Beliefs and world-views are subject to change based upon new experiences or evidence. Core values are not malleable and do not change with the job.

The Intersection of Values and the Democratic Rule of Law

Sacred Leadership recognizes and understands the distinct relationship between values and the democratic rule of law. We are a nation built on laws. Generally, those laws represent the will of the majority while protecting the individual rights of the minority. Over the decades, the rule of law has served our country and many others well. There are checks and balances in our system. We are also becoming a global community that increasingly respects the rule of law through the use of treaties and agreements reached through rule-making entities like the United Nations, the World Bank and others.

Invariably, leaders are confronted with legal conflicts that impinge upon their decision-making ability. More often than not, the conflicts are about decisions between choices, all legal, which may lead to very different ends.

To illustrate my point, consider the continuing debate about the legality of using enhanced interrogation techniques on terror suspects. Some opine that the techniques are legal. Others argue that they are not legal in accordance with either U.S. or international law. In this situation, like many others, leaders are confronted with matters that fall within the gray areas of the law. Of all the examples in this book, this illustration has engendered the most heated feedback, with people supporting both sides of the issue. I would not be surprised if, as you read this, you are joining that debate now! I hope this example helps you understand the complexity I am describing.

Sacred Leadership deals with these gray areas by referring back to purpose and to the principle of shared and enduring values. *Sacred Leadership* follows a two-part process. Leaders first ask if the decision, though legal, is consistent with their mission of serving the greatest good *and* secondly, if the decision is congruent with their personal and organizational values. If not, another solution must be found. In the case described above, if I were the decision-maker, the decision would not be simple, but it would be easy for me to make. My personal values of compassion, integrity, respect and honesty prevent me from condoning torture. Whenever faced with this kind of complexity and uncertainty, the leader can apply this two-part test.

Summary

The second principle of *Sacred Leadership*, respecting and honoring our shared and enduring values, governs our behavior and guides us through professional, legal, ethical and moral conundrums to make decisions with which we and others can live.

Chapter 4 Questions for Reflection

1. What are your core values as an individual? Try a values inventory.[47]

2. What do your values look like in action? Describe them in behavioral terms. The following statements may help you respond to this question:
   a. I know I am operating from the value of
      _____ when I _____.
   b. I know I am *not* operating from the value of
      _____ when I _____.

3. What are the values of your organization? How do you know?

4. As a leader, how do you communicate your company's values throughout the organization?

5. Based on your behavior, how would your employees, clients and customers define your organizational values?

6. How do your organizational values influence your hiring process?

7. How do your values influence your allocation of resources?

8. How do you insure that your self-interests do not get in the way of serving the greatest good?

9. Whose interests have you ignored?

10. How aligned are your personal values with those of your organization? Where are they in conflict? If they are in conflict, what will you do about it?

11. How can you improve, grow and develop in relationship to the concepts discussed in this chapter?

"Never doubt that a small group of thoughtful, committed people can change the world. Indeed, it is the only thing that ever has."[48]

—Margaret Mead

Chapter 5

ENLISTING, ENGAGING AND SUSTAINING

The Third Principle of "Sacred Leadership"

The third principle of *Sacred Leadership* is enlisting and engaging others and sustaining their involvement in achieving the mission. With the third principle we begin to weave a leadership tapestry using the threads of sacred purpose and values to enlist, engage and sustain others' commitment to the mission and the journey.

This chapter also reinforces the key point that *Sacred Leadership* is primarily about leadership not the individual leader. Because mission and values form the basis for enlisting and engaging others, *Sacred Leadership* is not dependent on the charisma or skills of the leader alone. After all, no one person (leader) can embody all of the attributes required to fulfill a mission of serving the greatest good. Rather, shared purpose and values, embodied in the mission, serve as beacons that attract others, enlisting them and engaging their diverse talents and skills in service to the mission.

My mother intuitively knew the power of this third principle and the way it wove purpose and values tightly together. Through her determination (probably one of her most potent values), she showed me how the power of intention led to possibility, which led to vision, which in turn led to reality.

My mother came from a very poor family background. Both of her parents were orphans and uneducated beyond third grade; her mother never learned to write. My mother grew up on a farm without running water, indoor plumbing and for many years no electricity.

From this humble background she emerged with her high school diploma and a longing to attend college – at a time when even wealthy women seldom had the opportunity. While she never realized her dream of college, my mother made it clear that my sister and I were "to go to college and amount to something." Her purpose and vision, for us to amount to something – to be something more – coalesced into a mission of getting her children to college. Her values of determination, persistence, courage and commitment all supported her in achieving that mission against all odds.

From my earliest memories, this intention was ever-present in my life. Neither she nor my father knew how it was going to happen, but she enlisted me in the dream and engaged me in the possibilities that could emerge from that dream (I wanted to be a scientist!). She enlisted my teachers (as early as second grade) to help me overcome my innate shyness and actively engage me in the learning process. And finally, she sustained my commitment even when she met with resistance. College just became an expectation, a possibility both my sister and I were to live into.

My understanding of the third principle germinated from this early experience. Throughout my professional life I have observed the negative consequences when the third principle is ignored. However, I have also experienced the way in which this third principle can transform the power of sacred purpose and values into action through others. The stories that follow illustrate both perspectives.

A Choice – The Cult of Victimhood vs. Enlisting and Engaging in Possibility

A common approach in organizations is one in which the leader presents a vision and persuades, cajoles or even threatens followers to buy into it. In part, this explains the passiveness we experience in so many employees today. I call this the cult of victimhood. We have become almost childlike in our expectations that leaders must know all of the answers (they can't) and solve all of our problems (impossible) as though we are helpless children. When they can't meet our expectations we feel powerless and if we don't step up as individuals, we soon begin to perceive ourselves as victims.

This was brought home to me in a recent conversation with my strategic partner in Munich, Germany. We were discussing the global economy and she said, "Why do Americans expect so much from their leaders? How can you expect the President to solve all the problems? Don't the American people know that no one person can deal with the complexity in the world today?"

In fact, many leaders like to reinforce the idea that they are the "know all/be all" answer to our problems, and as such, they feel there is no need to engage their followers (children) in the decision-making process.

The public sector example below illustrates the way in which the above attitudes and perspectives can play out in real life.

Revolving Doors and "Vision Burnout"

The average tenure of superintendents in large urban school districts is less than three years. Generally, they either are fired as a new school board is elected, or they move on to higher-paying jobs.

Superintendents are often charismatic and come to the new job with great and exciting visions for the kids, teachers and community. Through their charisma, they are able to gain the support of many key stakeholders and convince them to buy into their vision. However, because they know their tenure on the job will be short, they rarely take the time to enlist and engage the majority of their constituents in the leadership process. Their vision is usually developed in isolation, without a deep understanding of the inherent possibilities that exist in the system or within the individuals in the system.

Whatever those possibilities may be, they are too often lost.

Because these superintendents don't stay, the vision is not sustained. The organization experiences not only a revolving door of superintendents, but also of visions. This leads to "vision burnout," cynicism and low morale, which in turn leads to low productivity. Ask most teachers about the new superintendent's vision and you'll hear, "Been there, done that; this too shall pass." The result is that many employees are just going through the motions rather than being engaged with their deeper purpose. They feel they are victims of the system. Unfortunately, in this story, the students and their communities have the most to lose, yet almost no voice in changing it.

This scenario also plays out in the private sector. We watch well-known CEOs move from one company to another, leaving a trail of devastation and job losses in the name of short-term profits. Former Merck CEO Ray Gilmartin wrote that "it seems as though CEOs are recognized, and rewarded handsomely for downsizing and outsourcing, acquiring or merging and making the quarter – all justified by the responsibility to maximize shareholder value. Any of these actions can be necessary in certain circumstances...My concern is that these actions have become the standard by which CEOs are expected to manage."[49]

The story that follows shows the dramatic effect of making the choice to enlist and engage others – making the third principle the antidote to the "cult of victimhood."

"Getting the Air Right"

A colleague runs a privately-held firm that manufactures and distributes sophisticated electrical connectors.[50] In July 2009, during the height of a major recession, the company shipped a record $27 million in product. This high level of performance generated $1 million in incentive checks to be shared by all of his employees. During that same month, his two competitors suffered their worst month ever, issuing record *severance* checks.

The CEO maintains that the "employees magically created" the incentive dollars and "paid themselves" while allowing the company to generate record profits during very difficult financial times. The CEO's intention was to create an environment in which he enlisted and engaged his employees in the success of the company and by doing so created new and powerful possibilities for both the company and its individual employees.

The CEO explained that the corporate environment exhibited four traits:

1. Equality – Treating workers always with fairness and respect, exhibiting no favoritism or exploitation, with proper reciprocation in all things.
2. Recognition – Listening and paying personal attention to each individual, showing proper appreciation in financial and non-financial terms and creating the feeling they are members of an elite group that have a powerful influence on the success of the company.
3. Security – Clearly communicating what's going on, a stable, consistent set of ground rules and a real commitment to keeping the team intact – everybody comes home.
4. Opportunity – Ensuring they never feel stifled, that they feel they have an ongoing shot at fulfilling their dreams.

Through his leadership, this CEO enlisted and engaged employees at a level that produced record shipments against the odds. A majority of his employees were blue-collar workers and they were just as free to innovate and improve upon processes as were their colleagues who were engineers and scientists. They were allowed to cross boundaries to assist when their peers in other departments needed help. The results of their hard work, collaboration and creativity in improving productivity and efficiency throughout the company showed up in their paychecks as well as in the pay of the owners and executives. They felt that they were respected and that they were seen as valued members of the team.

When I walked the shop floor it was clear that employees were engaged and even enthusiastic about their work. When we stopped to speak with several of the workers it was also clear to me that the CEO knew them not only as employees but also as individuals.

The employees enlisted their trusted family and friends to fill vacancies. The CEO commented that they spent very little on recruiting and that turnover was extremely low. There were few disciplinary problems because everyone had a stake in the company's success.

He said, "Outsized income levels make employees the 'Godfathers' of their extended families." The work environment and the incentive plan engaged the employees in such a way that as the profits increased, their paychecks increased, usually exceeding those of their friends and neighbors. They often became the most successful and respected people in their families and neighborhoods. This changed the way they saw themselves and opened new possibilities in their lives. Many became homeowners while others sent their children to college. Some were able to do both.

His vision created a space in which his employees could realize the possibilities inherent not only in their jobs, but also in their larger lives. He did not define their possibilities; he created the opportunity for them to arise.

Imagine the power, responsibility and accountability employees feel as they have the opportunity to create these possibilities anew each month. By building the four traits into the work environment, the company grew a high morale culture. The CEO called it, "getting the air right."

The company built an environment of engagement that overtime sustained itself. The company's vision and the visions employees had for their individual lives became intertwined and sustained each other.

The Possibility in Participation

Part of the power of *Sacred Leadership* lies in its ability to believe in, nurture and uncover the inherent possibility within individuals in the organization, as well as, within the collective consciousness of the organization itself. This is a very different type of leadership when compared to our traditional conceptions and is especially powerful in the non-profit, public and social service sectors. Adam Kahane wrote, "Highly complex problems can only be solved using processes that are systemic, emergent and participatory."[51] In the context of the third principle, the key word here is *participatory*. The possibilities inherent in the future can only emerge by tapping into the dreams, aspirations, talents and gifts of the people we lead. Others must be enlisted and engaged if we are to successfully fulfill our mission.

The role of the leader changes within the context of *Sacred Leadership*. First, the leader helps others see the possibilities inherent in the mission to serve the greatest good. The leader enlists them in both possibility thinking and living. Think back to the blue-collar workers described earlier. Their commitment to the possibilities at work influenced the possibilities they saw could emerge in their personal lives. The CEO applied the third principle with powerful results. He lived the values and principles he espoused always treating his employees with respect. At that same time he provided compensation that supported their individual hopes and dreams.

Adapting the Third Principle – Special Cases

Not all situations allow for the immediate application of the third principle. Unfortunately, many people want to hold their leaders accountable for their daily lives, refusing to accept responsibility for their own participation in creating the problems they are encountering. This is the blind spot we are so often confronted with early in the enlisting phase. They say, "Why should I enlist in this mission? It is your (the leader's) responsibility to fix things for us." You can see them stuck in the old problem-solving paradigm, as well as in the cult of victimhood. The leader has an integral role in shining a light on this blind spot and changing patterns of beliefs – thus moving followers from victimhood to responsibility and accountability. Leaders are better able to perceive this blind spot because of their highly developed sense of self-awareness which we will discuss in Chapters 6 and 7.

Enlisting others becomes more difficult in these situations, especially in communities and organizations where hope has been extinguished by extreme poverty, despair or incompetence, or in those that are overwhelmed by chaos and violence.

Sacred Leadership uses a different initial approach in these situations. The two examples that follow highlight how the application of the third principle had to be adapted in response to these special cases.

The first case involves an environment steeped in despair and victimhood and required approaches that drew people into the conversation prior to enlistment and engagement. Often many in these communities do not have the communication skills or sophisticated language and processes to begin the journey alone.

The following story illustrates the first special case drawn from our work in the blighted urban core of Detroit.

The Dream Garden Emerges
In the fall of 2007, my wife and I were part of a group called

Menlo Lab, founded by Tracy Huston, a well-known international leadership consultant. Menlo Lab was named after the famous New Jersey laboratory of Thomas Edison, in which so many new discoveries and innovations were born.

Our goal was the development and implementation of new social technologies that would lead to large-scale, sustainable social change. On one such project, we worked with a local community in the heart of Detroit. This neighborhood presented a first impression that was deceptive. As we drove through the neighborhood, we encountered large old homes on tree-lined streets. This neighborhood had once been prosperous and beautiful. On closer inspection, however, a different picture emerged. About one of every three homes on any given block had been looted for copper and other valuables or burned to the ground. Hundreds of vacant lots, where homes once stood, were now filled with trash and overgrown with weeds. Similar neighborhoods could be found throughout this area of Detroit.

A few local community leaders and residents were trying to reclaim these vacant lots, turning them into urban gardens and small "pocket" parks that would provide an oasis from the economic and psychological chaos of the area. We had come to assist those leaders. Our goal was not to come in and impose a vision, but rather to enlist those in the neighborhood in discovering or rediscovering the dreams and aspirations they had for themselves, their children and their community.

With support from local leaders, DTE Energy and Cigna Healthcare, we began with a project called "Dream Garden," designed to capture the dreams and aspirations of the local residents. My wife, a working artist, designed an installation art piece for a vacant lot located at a busy intersection. Volunteers and local residents cleared the lot of debris and weeds and planted new plants. We then installed large 4 x 8 foot sheets of plywood on posts throughout the garden and designed a path that meandered among these boards. On each of the boards, we stenciled hundreds of hexagonal shapes to form the cells of a honeycomb. My wife chose the honeycomb design because of lessons learned from her father, who kept bees. When the bee-keeper provides a pre-fabricated honeycomb, the bees move directly into the production of honey. They utilize the energy that would have been spent creating honeycomb cells to create excess honey. The honeycomb billboards were a place for collecting the dreams (honey) of the community. Those dreams not only spurred action, but also nourished the souls of others who saw them.

As mothers and their children came by the lot, we engaged them in conversation and asked about their dreams and aspirations for their children. As they spoke, we wrote their words in the honeycomb cells. The dreams became the "honey" on which new possibilities could emerge and thrive. As they left, they told their friends. Soon, other mothers arrived with their children.

After school was dismissed that afternoon, kids began to visit what was now being called "Dream Garden." The elementary children were the first to engage, writing their hopes and dreams in each of the cells. Then some of the older teens dropped by, and again engaged in conversation and recorded their thoughts. There was skepticism, cynicism and even anger among a few, but slowly, over the next few weeks, the community began to own the garden and the cells in the honeycomb filled with the dreams and aspirations of this neighborhood.

The honeycomb billboards provided an easily accessible method to draw people into the conversation prior to enlistment. A few natural leaders began to step up. They took responsibility for realizing a few of the dreams that spoke to them, fed their souls and their sense of possibility. As they gave words and energy to their intention, resources and connections from local government and corporations became available to support their work.

From one of those honeycomb dreams arose an urban garden that employed locals from the neighborhood, reconnected many young people with the earth, and provided organic produce for employees in local businesses. Not only had hope been born, but a new micro-economy had emerged!

It seemed that never before had anyone engaged these citizens in discussions about their hopes and dreams. Typically, they were the recipients of someone else's vision for their lives, accounting for the cynicism and anger that we experienced from a few. In the old leadership paradigm, people often speak about empowerment as though the leader could "give power" to people. This kind of empowerment usually means that people will be given resources to live a vision provided by the leaders or others who hold political or positional power, once again reinforcing the cult of victimhood described earlier.

The "Dream Garden" project in Detroit was an unusual and experimental tool designed to enlist the community and uncover the possibilities hidden in their neighborhood and it accomplished the job in this special case. There are many more sophisticated tools, such as the World Café[52] , that can bring structure to the dialogue that needs to take place in these situations.

As *Sacred Leadership* enlists individuals in the mission and engages them in sacred purpose, it also opens them to the possibilities inherent in their own hopes, dreams and aspirations.

From Chaos to Engagement

The second special case for adapting the third principle involves environments that are chaotic. These situations require a more direct approach – starting with a strong leader who must take unilateral action to quell the chaos and then move to *leadership* that enlists and engages others in the process. At first glance this seems to contradict earlier statements that our focus is on leadership and not the leader.

Chaotic environments require an exception to our approach at the outset, but this is only temporary.

In chaotic situations the leader does not have the time to convene others in discussion, deliberation and dialogue prior to taking action. In chaotic circumstances, the leader must wrench his or her followers from the grip of helplessness and the fight, flight or freeze response. In chaos the leader must clear the fog to reveal the possibilities for others to see, and then enlist and engage them in realizing those possibilities.

In 1986, I was appointed to my first high school principalship. At that time, I was one of the youngest high school principals ever appointed in Los Angeles. When I received the call, I told the regional superintendent that it must be a mistake, because I knew that I hadn't yet passed the principal's exam. At that time, there was a written exam for all candidates from which an eligibility list was developed. In theory, candidates were ranked on this list and appointments were made in order from top to bottom.

The school district had a special rule allowing candidates to be placed in administrative positions even if they weren't on the eligibility list. The idea was that some candidates had special skills and experience that made them uniquely qualified for particular positions. As it turned out, that rule was used to place me! By this time in my career, I had worked at four different schools with gang problems; I had also worked with some wonderful teams that were expert in reclaiming out-of-control schools. Needless to say, it wasn't a popular decision to place me ahead of those on the eligibility list. However, I accepted the opportunity and was excited by the challenge.

My high school sat in the middle of a predominantly white middle-class neighborhood near the ocean but right next to the northern runway of Los Angeles International Airport. Over the years, as the population of school children from the local community had diminished; other students were bused in to make maximum use of the space. By the time I arrived, the school was 65% African-American and 25% Caucasian. The remainder represented a mix of students of Hispanic and Asian descent. About half the bused-in students were from poor, gang-infested neighborhoods, while the rest were from solidly middle-class homes. The year before I arrived, racial tensions were high, and gang violence had escalated to the point where gangs had walked onto campus and terrorized kids and teachers in their classrooms. The local community was upset and scared by the shootings in the neighborhoods surrounding the school.

At my first administrative staff meeting, I met with my two assistant principals, my dean, and the head counselor. Everyone was cordial, but I could sense tension in the room. I was younger than the rest of my team by many years, and they all knew that I had not passed the eligibility exam. My male assistant principal lived in the community and had begun his career teaching in this school nearly 30 years earlier.

After my team shared their job responsibilities and perceptions about the school, I began to outline the actions I wanted to take the first day. I had a formula for taking back an out-of-control school and wanted to start the first day of school by meeting with the entire student body in the auditorium.

My assistant principal said, "No way! You can't do that; you can't bring all of the kids into the auditorium."

"Why not?"

"The last time we tried something like that, the place got out of control. These kids don't know how to behave. You are just asking for trouble!"

Now my temperature was rising. I'm sure it showed on my face. The rest of the team was quiet, but their silence made it clear that they agreed with him. I said, "Look, this is my school and no one can stop me from meeting with and talking to my kids. I am in charge and these kids will behave."

He just laughed. "Well, I can tell you that you will do it alone. The faculty will not stay in the auditorium and put themselves through another near riot!"

"Fine!" I said. "I just need the faculty to get the kids into the auditorium and in their seats. After that, teacheers are free to leave. Just make sure I have a microphone that works and that all the lights are on."

Well, I thought, I'm off to a great start.

The next day was a pupil free-day. The teachers returned from summer vacation, department meetings were held and the teachers prepared their rooms for opening day. I asked for a faculty meeting to introduce myself and to lay out my plans for the beginning of the year.

We gathered in the school cafeteria. The majority of faculty members looked like they were in their mid to late fifties. Most had been at the school for 20 or more years and longed for the days when the school was white, middle-class and served the neighborhood. They weren't bad people; the changes at the school had been difficult for them. Truthfully, the changes the school had undergone had not been handled well over the years.

The assistant principal introduced me with the following line: "I want you all to meet our new principal, Jim Davis. You know what they say, when your boss is younger than you, it's time to retire!"

Laughter broke out among the faculty. There was snickering and knowing nods of their heads. "Icy" did not begin to express the temperature in the room.

I stood up and simply said, "Thank you Doug. You may be right. There is a stack of retirement papers in the main office. Anyone here should feel free to pick one up." There was silence, but also a few laughs and smiles. I don't think I ever felt so alone.

I went on to explain my goals and to talk about the assembly I had planned for the first day of school. Sure enough, my assistant principal was right. Most of the faculty refused to cooperate with my plan other than getting the kids seated in the auditorium.

Fortunately, it was a Friday; the weekend never looked so good. I prepped and practiced the remarks I was going to make to the students all weekend and didn't sleep at all Sunday night.

On Monday, I arrived at school early to greet the students at the front gate as they entered campus. The morning was a mess. Although all expected students had been scheduled and could go directly to their classes, literally hundreds of new kids showed up to enroll. Lines were long and tempers short. For the first hour, we spent most of our time keeping the peace – then came second period and the assembly.

I was in the auditorium early checking the sound and lights. (There is nothing worse than having an auditorium full of kids with lights on the stage and the house lights turned down. For some reason, most administrators haven't discovered this!)

Things started off well. The kids came in, sat down and were reasonably quiet. Not bad for 1,500 adolescents on the first day of school. I smiled to myself.

Then, as though on cue, the staff left. I saw the kids look around, puzzled and surprised. I immediately picked up the microphone and walked to the front of the stage.

"Good morning, I'm Mr. Davis, your new principal. I was told that you don't know how to behave in an assembly, but I don't believe that. I told your teachers they could leave. I want to share some things with you about our school and the way things are going to be."

All eyes were on me – and it was dead quiet! "I am going to put the microphone down now. I know if you are all listening, I won't need it."

I delivered my comments without the microphone, outlining my expectations for the year without interruption or disruption. When I finished, I received a standing ovation; there was positive electricity in the air. As we walked outside for the morning break, the kids gathered around me, introducing themselves and saying how excited they felt about a new beginning. I was on top of the world!

(Later, I found out that several teachers, my assistant principals and deans had circled back into the auditorium. While I was with the kids, word spread among the faculty that "he pulled it off.")

Next came step two. As I mentioned earlier, there is a set formula for regaining control of a school. At nutrition (that's what the morning break was called), I went out to groups of students and introduced myself again. Some were hostile and uncomfortable as I came into their space. There seemed to be an unwritten rule that kids controlled some areas of the campus and adults others. Those boundaries did not exist for me. I was not honoring them. The school belonged to me. No areas were off-limits to the adults.

Finally, a tough young man challenged me. "Get out of here – I don't give a fuck who you are!"

I knew this would happen. The other kids in the area gathered around, watching. "Come with me!" I told him.

"Fuck you!" He started to run. I chased him. As he attempted to scale the chain link fence to leave campus, I grabbed him and brought him down hard on the asphalt. School security arrived and he was taken away, never to return (he was transferred to another school).

Earlier in my speech to the students, I explained how we should treat one another and that all were welcome as long as they left their gang-banging outside our campus. This young man didn't believe me, and I had to make an example of him.

Rumors ran wild. By the time I got to my office, parents were calling to say they heard I had been jumped and injured. I assured them that was not the case. I walked through the hallways so that faculty could see I was OK. The kids wondered, "Who is this new principal?" One thing was certain; no one questioned who was in charge now. The school was mine and the chaotic environment had been contained; but I was still standing at the intersection of colliding worlds – alone.

Where Worlds Collide

Walter Earl Fluker, Professor of Leadership Studies at Morehouse College, describes what he calls "standing in the intersection where worlds collide."[53] He asks us to imagine ourselves with eyes closed, standing in a busy intersection with cars speeding past in all directions. Brakes screech and horns honk. Chaos surrounds us. There are no stoplights or stop signs.

How do we get out of the intersection? It quickly becomes clear that we cannot walk out of the intersection alone. As the principal, I knew I needed to enlist the students, staff and community if I was going to survive this intersection of colliding worlds and rein in the chaos permanently. I could not do it alone.

The process begins with dialogue. The leader asks, "What's happening here?" Leaders observe, listen, learn and try to understand the present situation. Fluker says, "Every great leader who has brought about creative change and transformation has done so with a community of fellow voyagers who are organized around vision, mission and specific goals and strategies."[54] Through dialogue and deep listening, others feel heard, understood and powerful. In the process, trust begins to develop and followers willingly enlist and commit to the journey.

Enlisting Others

Having broken the cycle of chaos, I had to begin the transition to a different kind of leadership. Once the chaos is diminished the real work begins and that requires others – the leader can't do it alone. This transition is crucial. Too often leaders relish the rush of power they experience in conquering the chaos and hesitate to move to a more inclusive form of leadership that incorporates the third principle.

It was now time to move from my role as the "Lone Ranger" into a leadership role that was more inclusive of others. As the new behavioral standards were being set and discipline established, I began enlisting and engaging the vast majority of the students who weren't involved with the gangs. They felt doubly victimized by both the gangs and the impotence of the adults in their lives – adults who were supposed to be in charge. These students wanted a peaceful and safe school where they could learn and have fun. By my actions, beginning on day one, the students and teachers began to see that none of us were helpless. As the feeling of victimhood began to fade away, a new sense of power and possibility emerged.

I met with the elected leaders of the student council. Although they were wonderful kids, they did not have a great deal of influence over the larger student body. I asked who the informal leaders were and I found ways to connect with them individually and informally solicited their assistance and support.

Next, I invited the faculty advisor of the school newspaper into my office and explained my thinking. I enlisted her in my plan. "I want you to have the kids identify some issue that is important to them, one that I can fix," I said. "I want them to challenge me to step up to the plate, be successful and live up to the words I spoke at the assembly."

"Are you sure?"

"Absolutely! It just needs to be done tastefully and in the tradition of good journalism. I want this paper to represent the voice of the student body."

"You're on," she replied with a smile.

With that agreement, the school newspaper became a public forum for dialogue and engagement with the student body. It was the fastest way to reach all 1,500 students. Possibility was beginning to turn into reality.

About a week later, the next issue of the school paper was published. On the front page was a cartoon caricature of me (appropriate and very well done – a framed copy sits in my office today!) accompanying an article about the dark and crowded hallways. Most of the lights in the interior hallways of the classroom buildings were broken or burned out. It was very dark and the kids were intimidated walking to class. Most of the teachers were even afraid to stand at their doors. The article was well written and the challenge was more than fair.

I went to battle with the school district bureaucracy, which was notoriously slow in responding to maintenance issues. I also enlisted the help of my immediate supervisor to explain why it was so important to deliver to the kids and staff. Beyond the clear safety issue, my credibility as a new principal was at stake.

Fortunately, within about six weeks, the lights were repaired and everyone took notice. The students also felt a new sense of power over their environment. They now had a voice that was respected and heard.

Broadening Engagement

Having begun the process of enlistment and engagement within the school, my next major challenge was to expand engagement to the broader community beyond the school gates. An opportunity arose out of an incident at our first home football game. Unlike many of the schools in the inner city, we were still playing our football games on Friday nights. The varsity game usually ended around 10:00 p.m.

As the football stadium was emptying out onto the street, I heard a "Pop! Pop!" followed by screams. As we moved through the ensuing chaos toward the street, we came upon a young man, a known gang member, lying on the sidewalk in a pool of blood. He had been hit in a drive-by shooting. One of the police officers assigned as part of our security detail that night provided first aid while we waited for the ambulance to arrive. The young man was rushed to the hospital. Thanks to that police officer, he survived his wounds.

The school police dispatcher called my wife to say there had been a shooting and that I would be getting home late. Those were always tense calls, as she wondered if and when she would hear that I had been shot. I got home about midnight. As always, I stopped about a block from home, took a deep breath and let my body shake as the adrenaline began to drain from my system.

When I arrived at school on Monday morning, the phones were ringing off the hook with angry community members demanding that we end our football program. Of course, I couldn't do this. Giving in to the violence would only embolden the gangs. We needed to take a stand, not only against the gang violence, but more importantly for the majority of the school community who deserved the opportunity to experience high school football, a great American tradition. This decision was not easy. I would be responsible if someone else was injured or killed at a future game.

I called the captain at our local police station and explained the situation and my concerns. He agreed to attend a community meeting with me. I then called a local minister and asked if he would host the meeting at his church. I did not want the meeting held at my school. Gang violence is a community issue and I didn't want this identified as just a school problem.

The meeting was held a few nights later. The church was packed with angry community members; the tension in the room was palpable. I was standing on the stage with the minister and the police captain. As I looked out over the audience, I opened my heart to them. These people had a good reason to be afraid. I realized I needed to shift the energy in the room if this meeting was going to be successful.

I went to the microphone, asked for everyone's attention, and introduced myself and the others on the stage. I opened by thanking everyone for coming in the spirit of dialogue and understanding. Rather than defend what had happened, I acknowledged their fear and frustration. The mood in the room began to shift and the tension subsided.

Through dialogue that evening, all voices and perspectives were heard and most were understood and respected. We agreed to meet again in working committees and over the next few weeks devised plans that saved the football program, but also greatly improved security for those attending the games, as well as for the neighborhoods surrounding the school.

Throughout the year, I continually found ways to enlist and engage students, staff and community in the possibilities inherent in our school. The process had its successes and failures, but we learned from each challenge as it arose. The school began to transform before our eyes.

In chaotic environments like this, the leader must establish a safe environment before all else. Next, the dialogue to uncover the possibilities for the school, students, faculty and community can and must begin. Chaotic environments usually require the leader to describe some picture for the future – usually a future with a very short time horizon in which the people can see the vision realized. However, as soon as things are under control, the leader must begin enlisting and engaging followers in uncovering their own dreams and aspirations. Only through such engagement can the commitment to the greatest good be sustained.

Who's On the Bus?

Most environments are not as challenging as America's inner cities and merely require an invitation to participate in a dialogue about possibility.

In his ground breaking study of America's most successful companies, best-selling author Jim Collins wrote, "The executives who ignited the transformations from good to great...first got the right people on the bus (and the wrong people off the bus) and then figured out where to drive it. They said, in essence, 'Look, I don't really know where we should take this bus. But I know this much: If we get the right people on the bus, the right people in the right seats, and the wrong people off the bus, then we'll figure out how to take it someplace great."[55]

It boils down to what Peter Block describes as the leader's role – to convene the right people and to ask the right questions.[56] *Sacred Leadership* defines the right people as those who already resonate with the mission, who are key influencers in the organization, who are respected by their colleagues and who have the skills and personal attributes to move the agenda forward, enlisting and engaging others along the way.

The process of enlisting others should be well thought out and planned. Who should be invited? Who will be first to the table? Who will be the most willing to engage? Who will be absolutely necessary for success? What are the natural networks within the organization that can be used to facilitate dialogue? What skills and talents do we need to ensure success on our journey? The questions are many, but necessary if we are to enlist and engage the right people at the right time.

Through dialogue and continuous learning, leaders are able to enlist those necessary to move to a deeper level of engagement.

While enlisting the right people is absolutely crucial, it is equally important to actively engage them in the work necessary to accomplish the mission. *Sacred Leadership* recognizes that there is no leadership without the "Do" – the work necessary to see possibility morph into tangible action.

Engagement requires a clear understanding from everyone about where the organization is headed, how the possibilities are translated into vision and how that vision fits into the larger context of the mission to serve the greatest good. Engagement involves the melding of great management and outstanding leadership to ensure that systems and processes are in place to make maximum use of physical, financial and human resources. *Sacred Leadership* demands rigor and maintains a laser-like focus on mission and values.

Sustaining Commitment

After people are enlisted and engaged, leaders focus on perhaps the hardest aspect of the third principle, sustaining commitment and engagement over time.

The "Dream Garden" story illustrates this difficulty. As we left the "Dream Garden" story, the enlisting and engaging of community sounded easy. But note that only a few of the hundreds of dreams deposited in the honeycomb were actually realized. In such desperate communities it takes much more effort to sustain the momentum over time. Much more needs to be done to understand the level of support needed to sustain commitment without stepping in and doing the work for the community – thereby reinforcing their feelings of powerlessness and victimhood. Time and resources need to be devoted to building local leadership capacity.

In retrospect, the "Dream Garden" project was not given sufficient time and energy to clarify the "sacred purpose" and identify shared values. This allowed other agendas to arise and forward momentum to be lost. No permanent leadership arose from within the community to enlist and engage others in realizing the dreams recorded in the honeycomb.

Perhaps we need to begin by carefully examining who we enlist in the beginning. This does not mean we enlist only people who think and act like us – that would be a mistake. However, we do not enlist everyone who comes to our door. To achieve our desired outcomes, we must be selective to insure that those we enlist believe in the mission, are committed to serving the greatest good, share common values, and possess the skills, talents and gifts needed in the moment. *Sacred Leadership* cannot compromise on these points.

People who own the mission, whose values are in alignment with the organization and their colleagues and who are using their own gifts and talents can usually sustain their own motivation and the work.

Sacred Leadership becomes absolutely crucial when progress stalls and morale starts to decline. Leadership helps buffer outside resistance so the team can focus on the work at hand. Through their words and actions, leaders sustain belief that change will come. When progress is difficult to see, they use their foresight, serving as scouts looking over the horizon – seeing a path here, a river blocking our way there and resources just over the next hill. They notice where course corrections may be needed. Their leadership helps sustain commitment and engagement during the tough times.

Leaders maintain ongoing dialogue within the organization and constantly scan and interact with the external environment. They study and evaluate the data, listen to their people and remain alert to blind spots. Leaders provide insight about what is working, and keep their minds and hearts open to what is not working and to new possibilities that might be emerging.

Roadblocks and Exhaustion

We have seen that poverty, hopelessness, violence and chaos can all make the implementation of the third principle most challenging.

The process of enlisting, engaging and sustaining is far more difficult in the public sector. Most public sector institutions are expected to serve whoever walks in the door (whether they want to be served or not!). In addition, the public sector has little control over who gets on the bus – and even less over getting the wrong people off the bus. I maintain that this is one of the reasons it has been so difficult to transform our public institutions. I do not say this to demean the many excellent public servants who work diligently every day. But Civil Service rules and union contracts often make it very difficult to implement this third principle of *Sacred Leadership* in the public sector and require much more of the leader's energy to get it right – energy that could be better directed at achieving sacred purpose.

Unfortunately, in far too many cases, leaders become exhausted trying to sustain commitment. Sometimes that exhaustion arises from the situations described above, but from my experience, I believe this exhaustion commonly results from three issues:

1. Leaders that are suffering from exhaustion usually do not have the right people on the bus. Their energy is drained by trying to keep people engaged and motivated.

2. Leaders often become exhausted doing the work of others who sit in the wrong seat on the bus – people that lack the knowledge and skills to effectively complete the job they have been assigned.

3. Exhaustion may also result from a vision derived from the leader, rather than possibilities that emerged from those being led. This is often true in organizations with purely charismatic leaders.

In Summary

In summary, the third principle of *Sacred Leadership* is about team and community. We have seen that the leader cannot succeed alone and that he or she must enlist and engage others in realizing the collective possibilities of the group.

Leaders know that commitment comes with individual (and organizational) engagement in realizing the possibilities emerging in the future. By engaging a future that has meaning in their lives and the lives of their organizations (family, church, business or company), followers become committed to seeing that future realized. When the leader has enlisted the right people, the team tends to be self-motivated, with commitment and engagement coming naturally.

Chapter 5 Questions for Reflection

1. Do you have the right people on your team?
   a. How do you know?
   b. If not, what are you going to do about it?

2. Do they occupy the right seat on the bus?

3. How do you enlist others in the mission of your organization?

4. How do you ascertain their commitment to the greatest good?

5. How do you engage your followers in possibility?

6. How do you sustain the energy and commitment of your team and others in your organization?

7. Do you find leading exhausting? Why? What will you do about it?

"Millions of ordinary, psychologically normal people will face an abrupt collision with the future...many of them will find it increasingly painful to keep up with the incessant demand for change that characterizes our time. For them, the future will have arrived too soon" [57]

—Alvin Toffler, "Future Shock"

Chapter 6

FORESIGHT –
SEEING AND PROVIDING
FOR THE FUTURE

The Fourth Principle of "Sacred Leadership"

The fourth principle of *Sacred Leadership* is providing for the future, while meeting the needs of the present. The fourth principle requires the leader to take both the short and long view. Foresight is a key tool for realizing this principle.

The Future Has Arrived Too Soon

This quote by bestselling author and futurist, Alvin Toffler is as applicable today as it was in 1970. As a species, we humans are used to the slow tide of evolutionary change. Historically, change happened over multiple generations, and individuals and societies were able to adapt. Not until the 20th century did we feel major acceleration in the change process, brought on primarily by the rapid innovation in technology. This was presaged by the arrival of the Industrial Age in the mid-19th century.

Take publishing, for example. Prior to the invention of the printing press, the written word was limited to a very small number of people. Books were reproduced by hand, primarily by monks in monasteries. The knowledge contained in those books was held by a very few elite business and religious leaders, as well as academics and patricians, who hoarded the books in private libraries and parted with their books like a miser parts with money.

Gutenberg's printing press, invented in the mid-15th century, changed that. With the ability to print books more economically and in greater numbers, far more people gained access to knowledge and information. His invention is credited with helping usher in the age of literary, artistic and scientific creativity that followed.

The printing press, with some improvements, was the predominant means of reproducing the written word for the next 500 years. Over that period, people and societies had time to adapt to this innovation and the amazing changes it birthed. Literacy rates soared in most western nations.

Changes precipitated by the development of word processing software in the late 1980s and early 1990s provide a sharp contrast to the gradual change experienced in previous centuries. In less than one generation, we have rocketed from the world of the printing press to the blogosphere, in which anyone can publish their work and distribute it to potentially millions (or billions!) of people around the globe with the push of a button.

For example, an Australian colleague recently published a new book. A new chapter was sent electronically every two weeks, accompanied by inquiries about my personal response to the material and my use of the techniques it contained. The book not only offered his knowledge and point of view, but also created a conversation between author and reader. I was allowed to set the price of the book based upon my ability to pay. If I were broke, it was perfectly acceptable to pay nothing.

Not only was this an innovative way to market, promote and gauge reader interest in the book; it also presented something the book publishing industry is loathe to entertain – a new, interactive approach to pricing. This new technology has appeared so quickly that the traditional New York-based book publishing industry has been knocked back on its heels, struggling with how to respond.

They have had no time to adapt their business models to accommodate this change, which seems to have occurred at the speed of light (or electrons).

This accelerating rate of change has been repeated in hundreds of ways in our daily lives, and is illustrated by our speed of travel (including its perils and discomforts), our telecommunications, our medical care and even the way we purchase and listen to music. We are bombarded with 24/7 real-time words and images with little or no respite, making the acceleration of change all the more stressful.

This exponential rate of change provides both promise and peril for leaders. There is the promise that these changes will help us do our sacred work more effectively and efficiently while serving more people.

The peril is that many of those we lead will become paralyzed by fear and their inability to cope with the rapidity of change. Like the Luddites of early 19th century England, who burned factories and their mechanized weaving machines, there are those today who rage against the exponential rate of change and attempt to resist it; however, they cannot stop its progress.

Not long ago, I visited a school where the person in charge of accounting for student body funds still kept her records in a written journal. She refused to learn and use spreadsheet or other accounting software! (Even more astounding was that she kept her job.) Too many people and organizations in our society have difficulty dealing with this change, both emotionally and psychologically. Indeed, for them, "the future has arrived too soon."

Resistance to these changes creates an unfolding drama, being played out in our daily lives, that locks us in a downward spiral of short-term thinking. We make decisions based upon past experience taking little note of the effect our decisions will have on the future, the lives of our children and the generations to come. The future will shape us with or without our input! This is why it is so important for leaders to focus their attention on the fourth principle.

Foresight

Leaders cannot provide for the future unless they can "see" it or at least make a good guess about what it may look like. This is why foresight is so important. When I speak of foresight, I do not mean that one predicts the future. The future cannot be predicted because there are far too many variables shaping it.

Foresight is the ability to imagine the possible and probable futures that might emerge, recognizing that *many* futures are possible. Foresight is not only sensing these possibilities but also understanding the driving forces and relationships shaping them.

Sacred Leadership requires that we act consciously in the present, while creating sufficient space to think about and plan for the future. Short-term actions combined with long-term vision based on foresight are not separate processes but are interdependent parts of the decision-making methodology.

The distinction between vision and foresight (what some call futuring) is important. The futurist Stephen M. Millett draws the distinction this way: "Futuring (foresight) looks at what is most plausibly, even likely, to unfold given trends, evolving conditions and potentially disruptive changes…Visioning, on the other hand, involves formulating aspirational views of the future based on what you want to see happen…."[58]

Sacred Leadership approaches foresight from both an organizational and an individual perspective. Organizationally, a planning process called Strategic Foresight provides a very structured approach for looking into the future. The individual perspective is more personal in nature and uses what I call Intuitive Foresight. It is important to note that these two perspectives inform one another, but they are more easily grasped by examining them individually.

Strategic Foresight

Strategic Foresight is a complex, analytical approach organizations can use to better grasp and plan for the future. It is a powerful tool in helping leaders predict and understand the incoming changes that will impact their organizations, as well as formulating the strategies through which they will attempt to influence the future. From an organizational perspective, it is important that leaders know that the Strategic Foresight process exists and I strongly urge leaders to employee its techniques when thinking about and assessing the future of their organizations.[59]

There are six major guidelines associated with Strategic Foresight:

- It begins with a process of **framing** in which we establish clarity about our mission, limiting the scope of our efforts to the issue at hand.
- The next step is **scanning** in which we look at the internal and external environment of the organization looking for data, trends, beliefs and assumptions that may affect us in the future.
- Scanning is followed by **forecasting** in which we analyze and use all of the data and trends we have collected to create probable alternative futures. Forecasting provides scenarios against which we can monitor our progress, look for leading indicators and maintain awareness of unexpected events (wild cards).
- The final three guidelines follow the more traditional processes of **visioning, planning,** and **acting** based upon the forecasts that were developed.

In summary, Strategic Foresight provides a set of probable futures (scenarios) for the organization as well as several alternative paths forward. The organization can then select the path it wishes to follow, aware that there are alternatives that can be considered as the environment changes.

A detailed description of Strategic Foresight is beyond the scope of this book. An excellent and very thorough description can be found in the book *Thinking about the Future: Guidelines for Strategic Foresight*[60] by Andy Hines and Peter Bishop.

At first glance, Strategic Foresight appears to be a very linear process, but remember that it becomes an even more powerful tool when it is informed by Intuitive Foresight.

Intuitive Foresight

In the late 1970s, I decided to pursue my doctoral degree and was accepted by the Graduate School of Education at the University of California, Los Angeles (UCLA). I attended evening classes while working full-time. My fellow students were an interesting and diverse group that represented a spectrum of ages, backgrounds and ethnicities and included several international students. The classes were excellent and the discussions almost always challenging and thought provoking.

After several years, I completed my course work and passed the grueling comprehensive exams. For my dissertation topic, I chose an idea that had interested and intrigued me for years, "The Role of Intuition in Leadership." It was at this point that my interests crashed head-on into an old prevailing paradigm. When I ran this topic by my advisor, he said, "This is soft stuff. It can't be measured. No one knows what intuition is!"

This was before the advent of the personal computer and instantly accessible search engines. The computer databases were small, very specialized and prohibitively expensive – especially for this graduate student. At that time, I could find nothing in the literature to support my assertion that intuition was a crucial component of leadership.

From my experience, it was crystal clear that intuition played a critical role in leadership and in dealing with individuals and groups. It was equally clear to my advisor that this topic was "nonsense," neither quantifiable nor suitable as a dissertation topic. He was not able to foresee the new paradigm evolving in the field of leadership development. It wasn't until years later, after the advent of modern computer search capabilities, that I learned that Robert K. Greenleaf had touched on the topic of intuition in his seminal essay on servant leadership. He wrote that essay in 1970 – nearly a decade before my graduate studies!

For most of my life, I have been able to anticipate and perceive life from a future perspective. Examples throughout this chapter illustrate how that skill continues to serve me today.

Another Sense?

Think you of the fact that a deaf person cannot hear.

Then, what deafness may we not all possess?

What sense do we lack that we cannot see and cannot hear another world all around us?

What is there around us that we cannot (sense)?[61]

Think of Intuitive Foresight as another sense as described in the quote above by science fiction writer, Frank Herbert, author of *Dune*. Intuitive Foresight is not a special gift imparted to some and not to others. It is often described as a "hunch" or "gut feeling" but it comes from a set of skills, knowledge and sensitivities that can be developed with deliberate practice. In fact, awareness of intuition goes back at least 2400 years to Aristotle. In his *Nicomachean Ethics*, Aristotle described intuition as one of the five ways of knowing truth.[62] However, it is not just science fiction writers and ancient philosophers that talk about intuition.

Bob Lutz, former President of Chrysler Corporation, described how he came up with the idea of the high performance Dodge Viper that many credit with the dramatic turnaround of Chrysler in the 1990s. When trying to describe how he made the risky decision to pursue the Viper, Lutz said, "It was this subconscious, visceral feeling. And it just felt right."[63]

Ralph S. Larsen, former Chairman and CEO of Johnson & Johnson, explained the importance he placed on intuition when promoting executives, "Very often people will do a brilliant job up through middle management...But then they reach senior management, where the problems get more complex and ambiguous, and we discover that their judgment or intuition is not what it should be. And when that happens, it's a problem; it's a *big* problem."[64]

For these and many other executives, Intuitive Foresight is another tool or personal attribute to draw upon to remain competitive in today's rapidly changing world.

Seeing Around Corners

Robert Bruner, the Dean of the University of Virginia's Darden School of Business, signaled the importance of Intuitive Foresight in an interview in the *Wall Street Journal*: "I think of leaders as having many attributes, but one of the key ones is self awareness. Good leaders are present and engaged and alert...This awareness is almost an *ability to see around corners*, a *capacity to look ahead*, think strategically and imagine consequences."[65]

Let me illustrate Bruner's point with two very different anecdotes, one from my first principalship and the other from my son, David, who loves to surf.

You're Everywhere!

Early in my first year as a high school principal in Los Angeles, I arrived at school at 6:00 a.m., 30 minutes earlier than usual. I still don't consciously know my reason for heading to work so early. As soon as I got out of the car, I felt something was wrong. I couldn't shake the feeling. Rather than proceed directly to my office to drop off my briefcase, my usual routine, I started walking the campus. This high school campus was particularly large, with 12 separate buildings situated on more than 50 acres. Within a few minutes I had walked directly to one of the classroom buildings, on which I found the exterior walls had been spray-painted with racial epithets and Nazi swastikas. I immediately got on my walkie-talkie (this took place during the pre-cell phone era) and called my custodial staff. After taking pictures, they painted over the graffiti just minutes before the first bus dropped off its group of African-American students.

What would have happened if those kids had arrived and been confronted with these hate-filled messages? I can only imagine. One thing is certain; my day would not have gone well.

What led me to arrive on campus early, forego my usual routine and find this graffiti? Some would call it luck, but I don't think so. It was what I now call Intuitive Foresight that allowed me to sense things in a different way. These kinds of occurrences took place all of the time when I worked in schools. My students often said, "Mr. Davis, you're everywhere!" I did employ some very specific techniques to be noticeable and to make my presence known on my school campuses, but I also had a kind of "knowing" when and where a problem was about to surface. Some of my colleagues said that I just had a "nose for trouble," something they didn't understand and couldn't explain. I called it intuition and it is a skill that can be developed.

Surfs Up

Here's another example. One day, when discussing Intuitive Foresight with my son, he said, "I know what you mean. It's like surfing. I usually stand on the shore and watch the waves come in for a few minutes. Then I paddle out on my board and at a certain distance I stop, turn and wait for just the right wave. Some of the guys paddle too soon and get in front of the wave; others start too late and miss the wave; but the good surfers just know and sense when to paddle, where to guide the board and end up on the crest of the wave and ride it into shore. The other guys ask, "How do you do that? How do you know? It's like magic, the way you almost always catch the wave!"

Do You Believe in Magic?

In both of these anecdotes, it may appear that something strange or supernatural happened. Why are some people always in the right place, on the right wave, knowing just where to go and what to do?

This isn't magic. It's foresight informed by intuition. When you experience Intuitive Foresight, you are no longer reacting to the future as it presents itself in your life, but rather, you become an active participant in shaping it.

The science fiction author, William Gibson, put it this way: "The future is already here, it is just unevenly distributed."[66] To those who are less aware, it does appear that you predicted the future. In reality, you are merely seeing and sensing indicators that others have missed. You are sensing something, and then acting upon it in ways others never considered.

Our brains are constantly taking in information of which we are completely unaware. Neuroscientist, David Eagleman, writes that "Almost the entirety of what happens in your mental life is not under conscious control..."[67] He likens our mental activity to an iceberg, the majority of which is hidden from view. This information comes not only through our five senses but also from other parts of our body, which are linked to our unconscious brain by our spinal cord and nervous system, through hormones in our circulatory system and through other forms we are only beginning to discover.[68]

Intuitive Foresight is difficult for some to grasp. Foreseeing the future sounds like something out of a fairy tale or science fiction book. Robert K. Greenleaf described it this way in his seminal work, *The Servant as Leader*: "The leader...needs to have a sense for the unknowable and be able to foresee the unforeseeable."[69] He goes on to say, "Prescience or foresight is a better than average guess about what is going to happen when in the future."[70]

This is not fortune telling. There are specific skills and attributes leaders can develop to improve their abilities to "see around corners."

Developing Intuitive Foresight

Nearly all of us can develop Intuitive Foresight; however, some people are innately more sensitive to the clues available to them and therefore are more accurate in what they see as they peer into the future. This is similar to the differences we observe in athletic prowess, musical talent or intellectual capacity. There is a range of ability in Intuitive Foresight as well. We all have some ability, but our level of expertise is distributed across a scale from low, to average, to high, to "over the top."

The six practices that follow provide a starting point for further developing your skill of Intuitive Foresight.

Anticipating Second and Third Order Effects

One of the skills necessary for the most basic form of foresight is the ability to anticipate the first, second and third order effects of our actions. For instance:

- I do X, then Y happens = First Order Effect
- Because Y happens, then Z occurs = Second Order Effect
- When Z occurs, I then experience A = Third Order Effect

If leaders take the time to anticipate, they will have the ability to fairly accurately see or predict what the second and third order effects of their actions will be, allowing them to plan accordingly.

However, it is important to note that major difficulties can arise when large distances of space and time separate the first action from the second and third order effects. In many cases, generations pass before we experience the third order effects of our actions. For instance, no one predicted that one third order effect of the Industrial Revolution that began in the 1700s would be the high levels of pollution now influencing our health as well as our global climate.

Finding Silence

We live in a hyper-connected world. This is especially true for leaders. Telephones, faxes, email, texts and smart phones keep us connected 24/7. How many of you sit in meetings where people are checking messages, leaving to take calls, surfing the Internet or nervously checking the clock? Larry Smarr, a professor at the University of California, San Diego, put it like this, "The meat is in the room, but the mind is somewhere else."[71]

Leaders are not exempt from this hyperactivity. However, taking a break from the incessant noise that intrudes on their lives, slowing down, stopping and finding a degree of silence, allows them to attend to their interior state. This grounds them and supports their success. They need time to reflect: "Who am I being in this moment? How is my being serving the greatest good and reflecting my values?"

Silence permits leaders to "see" and "sense" the present and opens them to the emerging possibilities of the future. If we are not careful, we can find ourselves moving so quickly that we disregard the present and miss the future. *Sacred Leadership* requires us to know how to avoid adopting what Jon Kabat-Zinn calls the "dance of inattention and instability of mind" and being "driven to distraction"[72] that often accompanies our fast-paced lives.

Finding silence takes discipline. Holistic health practitioner, Diane Dreher, offers the simple practice that follows for bringing more silence into your life. Think how often you walk into a room and turn on the radio or television. She writes that, "This background chatter makes it less likely that you will meditate, read, work creatively or attend to your own thoughts. Silence returns us to ourselves and our natural rhythms.

- The next time you automatically turn on the radio or television ask yourself why.
- If you choose to watch or listen, leave it on. If not turn it off.
- Make silent periods an important part of your day. You may miss out on some of the local news, or sitcoms, but you'll become better acquainted with an old friend – yourself."[73]

Exercises like this and practices such as meditation, yoga, etc.[74] help leaders pause, reflect and see and sense differently, from a new space of calm mindfulness. Within this space, Intuitive Foresight develops. We move from reacting to the past into a place where we begin to shape the future.

Seeing your Seeing

"Seeing your seeing"[75] is a crucial attribute and an important skill that allows leaders to see more broadly and from a higher perspective. *Sacred Leadership* requires leaders to suspend judgment and maintain open minds whereby they can entertain many more possibilities. Suspension requires that we expose our reactions, impulses, feelings, assumptions, beliefs and opinions so that we notice them, give them our attention and try to understand how they are influencing our perception.

Suspending judgment does not mean that we never judge. It is a practice of suspending judgment as long as possible – allowing us to see without looking through the potentially distorted filter of our judgment. Our ability to see expands as we suspend judgment, allowing new knowledge, insight and understanding to open to us, informing our decisions and actions.

The goal is to operate from a space of open learning rather than a space of fixed knowing, thereby increasing the information and subtle signals that are available to inform our Intuitive Foresight.[76]

Deep Listening

Deep Listening is a skill focused on listening for understanding. Deep Listening not only changes us, but also causes a profound change in the person we're talking to because they feel heard and understood. That feeling of being heard often causes our hearts to open. As our hearts open, "seeing" expands. As we listen from our heart, our empathic understanding can dissolve our judgment and we can begin to move into relationship. Moving into relationship can allow trust to develop, cooperation to emerge and agreement to come within our grasp.

Although Deep Listening requires some training and a lot of practice, the tips that follow describe some skills that you can practice now:

- Listen and read in the spaces between the words and lines; sense what isn't being said and try to ascertain why.
- Look at breathing patterns, emotions and patterns of distraction and try to determine their cause or ask the person if your perceptions are correct.
- Pay attention to speech patterns that emerge – is the speech agitated, hesitant etc.
- Look for a reticence to speak and probe to understand.
- Determine what is being communicated by other's body language. Is their body language consistent with their words?

Deep listening moves us from just hearing what is being said, to informing our Intuitive Foresight by picking up signals that others may miss, allowing us take action proactively.[77]

Intuitive Sensing

You can sharpen your sense of intuition by some of the practices listed on the following page:

- Be present. Pay attention and maintain a 360°/top to bottom, inside/out view of your environment.
- Become aware of the senses you are using to gain awareness. Expand your way of observing. What do you know is happening and how?
- Be aware when you sense anger, tension, happiness, sadness or other emotions in yourself and in others.
- Pay attention when the hair on the back of your neck stands up. If you sense something is there, check it out. Even though you may not be correct, honor this sense. The more you honor and practice this intuitive way of knowing, the more precise it becomes.

Cross-Indexing

Cross-Indexing is a sophisticated approach to building our Intuitive Foresight by expanding the breadth and variety of knowledge available to us when thinking about the future. Alden Hayashi, writing in the *Harvard Business Review*, maintained that "The ability to see similar patterns in disparate fields is what elevates a person's intuitive skills from good to sublime."[78] You can begin this process by:

- Reading books and periodicals outside of your personal and professional areas of interest.
- Networking with people outside of your profession and with those whose interests differ from yours.

Choice Making

The fourth principle of *Sacred Leadership* requires that we are aware of what is happening in the present – and what might happen later. This awareness helps us perceive positive signals as well as unexpected events, allowing us to quickly recognize meaningful changes and adapt to them. As leaders, we do not have to wait passively for events to occur. We know, as Joseph Jaworski wrote, that if we operate from "possibility rather than resignation, we can create the future into which we are living, as opposed to merely reacting to it when we get there."[79]

When leaders begin to shape the future through their decisions, actions and the allocation of resources, they operate in a constant state of "choice making." Each choice affects and changes the future either positively or negatively – consciously or unconsciously.

In order to serve the greatest good, we must insure that our choices create a positive future. One that is livable, sustainable and better than the world in which we live today. In a real sense, we must build a world that we want our great grandchildren to inhabit and experience. This harkens to the well-known precept of the Iroquois Indians, whose chiefs consciously tried to peer seven generations into the future when making major decisions. The fourth principle helps leaders do that.

Chapter 6 Questions for Reflection

1. Where in your life has the "future arrived too soon"? Be specific.

2. How developed is your foresight? Why do you believe this?

3. How do you honor your intuitive nature? Do you trust it?

4. How is your past influencing your "seeing"?

5. How does your "knowing" influence your "seeing" in the present?

6. How can you suspend judgment and move from a "knowing space" into a "learning space"?

7. How open is your heart space? Would others agree?

8. How is your choice-making shaping your future today?

> *"We need to be the change we wish to see in the world"* [80]
>
> —*Mahatma Gandhi*

Chapter 7

SKILLS AND ATTRIBUTES
REQUIRED FOR THE
PRACTICE OF
SACRED LEADERSHIP

Sacred Leadership derives its power to transform and shape the future through the collective. *Sacred Leadership* is not an isolated task; it is a group endeavor in which leadership and followership are of equal importance. *Sacred Leadership* is not about the knight in shining armor, but rather it is more akin to the knights of the round table. That being said, someone has to get things moving, usually an individual or small group of individuals. They articulate the values and mission and begin the enlisting process described in Chapter 5. These are the leaders that step up and begin the process that allows *Sacred Leadership* to emerge.

I am often asked if specific skills and attributes are required for these leaders to be successful in initiating and sustaining the work. The answer is yes and this chapter highlights the skills and attributes that are most important.

This chapter is not meant to outline all of the skills and attributes of leadership. That would take volumes. All leadership requires the requisite management skills needed to run an organization, skills that are most often learned in school and on the job. All leaders also require a high level of emotional intelligence to be successful.[81] The skills and attributes I define in this chapter go beyond management skills and emotional intelligence. They are more personal, requiring purposeful individual growth and development over time. These skills and attributes are needed to enlist others and sustain a level of engagement so powerful that it can help shape the future. The nine key personal skills and attributes highlighted in this chapter enable *Sacred Leadership*.

Self-Awareness

We have an innate capacity for self-awareness; it passes to us through our genes and is vital for our survival. Even though self-awareness is innate, it seems that many have forgotten how to pay attention. Our capacity for self-awareness begins with the realization that we are unaware or unconscious in many areas of our lives.

Self-awareness is both internally and externally oriented. There is an awareness that is internally directed towards our emotional and physical state. This awareness asks how we are feeling and acting in the moment; it brings our feelings and actions to consciousness.

Our awareness is also directed out toward the external environment. We live in relationship and interdependence and our externally oriented awareness heightens our attention to what is going on with the people and world to which we are connected.

Our internally and externally directed awareness brings to our attention how our inner state is affecting our relationship to the larger environment and how that external environment is affecting our internal state.

The ability to develop our internally focused self-awareness gives us greater control over our emotional and physical reactions to the external world. Many of us have experienced a boss, colleague, or loved one whose emotions seemed to boil out of control with no way to turn down the heat. They scream, curse, yell and sometimes throw things. In the moment they seem to be completely unaware of their behavior. As the episode subsides, they often apologize saying that "I lost control, I was not myself." This is exactly what happened. In cases like this, their emotions have them rather than them having their emotions. The more primitive areas of their brains took over so quickly that their cognitive brain could not exert control.

What is needed in these cases is what Kwame Anthony Appiah describes as "an exercise of reason, not just an explosion of feeling."[82] Developing self-awareness allows us to "see" our cognitive brain about to be hijacked by "the explosion of feeling." This awareness allows us to "exercise reason" beforehand and gives us greater control over our response. Lennick and Kiel wrote that conscious awareness allows us to "choose what we think, what to think about and how to think about it. We can also choose what we do and what we say."[83] Therefore, our internally focused self-awareness allows us to shape our thoughts, feelings and actions rather than being shaped by them.

Our externally oriented awareness is equally powerful; however, we often don't realize just how blind we are to what goes on around us. Jon Kabat-Zinn, professor at the University of Massachusetts Medical School, put it this way, "I'm afraid many of us go through our lives unaware or unconscious to that which surrounds us. We die without ever having lived…it is about paying attention in your life as if it really mattered…."[84]

As mentioned in Chapter 6, a large part of our mental activity and awareness operates at an unconscious level. Of course, this is not unexpected. We would not want to have to think to make our hearts beat, our lungs breathe and our foods digest. We have also experienced this unconsciousness in a very real way when we arrive at work, having no recollection of the details of our drive. We operated as though we were on automatic pilot and, in fact, we were!

We often don't realize just how much we have turned over to our unconscious mind. Eckhart Tolle, author of *A New Earth: Awakening to Your Life's Purpose,* put it this way: "…thinking without awareness is the main dilemma of human existence."[85] Rather than being mindful of our surroundings, we have become mind-less. It is this mind-lessness, which requires leaders to also develop a self-awareness that is externally oriented. For example, try to answer the following questions: What color was the car parked next to you as you arrived at work today? What color are your colleague's eyes – yes, the one you've worked with for the past five years? What team member is not feeling up to par today? These are, in many ways, superficial examples, but they exemplify the way in which we are unaware of or automatically ignore information. You probably noticed all of these things today, but they never made it to the level of conscious awareness. What else did you miss today that may, in fact, affect your success as a leader?

Our ability to maintain high levels of self-awareness is important because our current position in life has been determined, in large measure, by where we focused (or didn't focus) our attention and awareness in the past. If our awareness is focused and conscious, we are able to deliberately act in the moment and influence our unfolding future. However, if we are not aware and conscious of our present circumstances (both internal and external), our future unfolds by chance and we often look back, feeling regret for our past choices. Rather than shaping our future, we become casualties of our unconscious past.

Self-awareness is about suspending judgment and opening our awareness to all that is present in the moment, seeing the filters of our beliefs, judgments and emotional responses. We can't lose these filters, but we can get better at noticing them and the way they impact our awareness and experience. As we open our awareness, we develop a new level of discernment, which allows us to see new relationships, interconnections and possibilities that are present in the moment, possibilities that might otherwise have gone unnoticed.

Jon Kabat-Zinn further illuminates this point when he writes,

Discernment…as differentiated from judging, leads us to see, hear, feel and perceive infinite shades of nuances, shades of gray, between all white and all black, all good and all bad, and this, what we might call wise discerning, allows us to see and navigate through different openings, whereas our quick-reaction judgments put us at risk for not seeing such openings at all and missing the full spectrum of the real and thus lead us to automatically and unwittingly limit the possible.[86]

I was recently involved in a meeting with a client that illustrates this point. We were listening to a rather disjointed proposal from someone seeking a partnership. Despite the poor presentation, I felt that there were many possibilities worth pursuing that would support my client's plans for the future. However, it wasn't immediately clear in what direction we should move and my client cut the meeting short and broke off further discussions.

As we debriefed the meeting, my client critiqued the presentation, made judgments about the motivation of the presenter and basically "wrote off" any possibility of a partnership. My client allowed his awareness, and his ability to listen, to be clouded by a rush of judgments and opinions. His willingness to succumb to his immediate judgments limited his ability to see and therefore limited his freedom of choice in the future.

Self-awareness as a leadership attribute takes on additional importance because the leader's awareness is integral to awakening awareness in others. As the leader models self-awareness and brings it to group consciousness, self-awareness is raised throughout the organization.

Raising your level of self-awareness requires deliberate and conscious practice. Each of us must find our own technique or personal practice that helps us attain higher levels of self-awareness. As a start, throughout the day, pause, reflect and answer the following questions:

1. Present Moment: What am I thinking, feeling, experiencing and doing now, in the present moment? How are these shaping my awareness?
2. Others' Reactions: In this moment, how are others reacting to my thoughts, feelings, and actions?
3. Anticipating: Am I anticipating the impact my thoughts, feelings and actions will have on others?
4. The Problem: Are my thoughts, feelings and actions part of the problem(s) we are experiencing?

Empathy

Empathy grows out of our capacity for self-awareness. When we feel empathy we become aware of and actively engage in another person's feelings. For instance, when my mother died a few years ago, several of my friends who had never met her came to her funeral. It was clear to me that through empathy they were feeling the same grief I was feeling, even though they had no personal connection to my mother.

From a leadership perspective, empathy builds group cohesion and loyalty by improving communication and understanding. Popular social thinker, Jeremy Rifkin, wrote, "Comfort and compassion between people creates good will, establishes the bonds of sociality and gives joy to people's lives. Much of our daily interaction with our fellow human beings is empathic because that is our core nature. Empathy is the very means by which we create social life and advance civilization."[87] Therefore, empathy plays a key role in our ability to enlist, engage and sustain others' commitment to the sacred mission as discussed in Chapter 5.

Empathy researcher Martin Hoffman proposes that the "…capacity for empathic affect, for putting oneself in another's place, leads people to follow certain moral principles….Empathy underlies many facets of moral judgment and action."[88] In this way, empathy also supports the values based approach of *Sacred Leadership*.

As we lead people to the mission of serving the greatest good, empathy becomes one of what Rifkin calls "the thread(s) that weaves an increasingly differentiated and individualized population into an integrated social tapestry, allowing the social organism (and the organization) to function as a whole."[89]

Creating a Gap and Finding Stillness

The ability to create a gap between stimulus and response, and move into stillness is another key skill required for *Sacred Leadership*. This ability compliments the skill of "Finding Silence" discussed in Chapter 6. In today's fast-paced leadership environment, leaders are asked and expected to act instantaneously. Leaders need to resist this pressure whenever possible, by minimizing their reactive stance, and learning to create a gap between perception, interpretation, understanding and action. That gap is created through our self-awareness – our awareness that we are being pressured and that we can stop and take time to consider. The greater the gap, the greater our control and influence over the choices we are about to make.

Creating mental and physical space for stillness and deep reflection is a key, not only for opening oneself to possibility, but also for sustaining focus and energy for yourself, your followers and the organization as a whole. There is no one practice that works for everyone. What is important is to find the practice that works for you.

I begin each day with a ritual, which I instituted nearly twenty years ago. We have a window seat that overlooks our garden and the city of Los Angeles. I sit quietly, letting my thoughts come and go – not attending to any of them. I become aware of how I am feeling, both physically and emotionally. Solutions and understanding of problems solved in my sleep slowly seep into my consciousness. Over time, the patterns and possibilities of my day begin to emerge. My attitude, how I will approach the day, is set in a quiet and open manner. Note that it is all a matter of choice – my choice!

After years of practice, I can now move into that mental space within a few seconds, and in almost any place. In that space, I am aware of my thoughts and feelings and the way in which I am experiencing the moment. I am conscious of the actions I am about to take. If judgment, cynicism and fear appear, I quickly adjust, let go and move into understanding, empathy and possibility. In that moment, I can change my energy and the energy of those around me, creating a space where dialogue and understanding can emerge.

We have all found that space at times in our lives – especially as children. If you can't find it now, don't worry; it is not lost. It simply requires that you remember.

I rediscovered that silent space while gardening, returning to the earth. As I work in the soil, my senses change, open and expand. My pulse slows and my mind calms and wonders, floating from soil to plant to sky and back again.

Once you have rediscovered your silent space, try to re-create it and the feelings that accompanied it. Pay attention to what helped you move into that space. For years, I kept a picture from one of my favorite backpacking trips in Yosemite on my desk. Before or during a difficult situation, I would glance at the picture and remind myself how peaceful and connected I felt in that moment. From that internal space, I would enter the difficult situation differently, from a perspective of peace, understanding and possibility, and with the intention of creating a new positive future outcome rather than solving an old problem from the past.

Intuition and Synchronicity

As discussed in Chapter 6, intuition is another skill required for *Sacred Leadership*. Our bodies and minds are sensory instruments. Early in our evolution, our senses, including our intuition, were attuned to our environment in subtle ways that many of us have lost or at least have allowed to atrophy over time.

This atrophy was highlighted while traveling with an experienced guide in Tanzania. He would intuitively know where to look and then, in the distance, he would see animals that we could not see until he pointed them out as we looked through our binoculars. His eyes were attuned to patterns in the landscape and could detect subtle breaks in the pattern, even when the animals were camouflaged. However, a week into our safari, we began to gain a new acuity in our seeing, or perhaps we were regaining our old acuity that had deteriorated with lack of use.

I believe the same is true with all of our senses, including our intuition. As we pay attention to our intuition, we begin to see differently. We see new patterns and experience new ways of knowing. I am not saying to always trust your intuition any more than you always trust your other senses. However, intuition does provide an added dimension to our understanding of the world.

An interesting thing happens when we become aware of and pay attention to our intuition. The world becomes clearer. It is like seeing with a new set of glasses, creating clarity where there once was fog.

Also, as we take notice of our intuitive insights, we begin to experience an increase in synchronistic events. Carl Jung described synchronicity as "…a meaningful coincidence of two or more events, where something other than the probability of chance is involved."[90]

Most of us have experienced synchronicity, although we may have called it something else. While sitting down to write this chapter, I was thinking about a principal with whom I used to work. I hadn't seen her for nearly 15 years and we only correspond during the holiday season. Two days later, I was visiting a client – and there she was! She lives hundreds of miles away and this was her first visit to my client's workplace. During our conversation, I learned that she was in the process of developing a leadership program. As I began describing *Sacred Leadership*, she said, "This is just what I've been looking for!" I don't know what will happen following this encounter, but I do know that a new possibility exists for practicing my work.

I cannot explain such synchronistic events, but I do know that leaders should not view these events as interesting coincidences. It is important to look within the coincidence and seek the meaning, purpose and possibility to be found in these "chance" encounters.

Synchronicity is the universe's way of saying, "Pay Attention! This is what you need." Over the years, I have found that, if I am paying attention, what or who I need is usually just around the corner.

Intuition and synchronicity provide leaders with new and different information, thereby opening new doors to understanding and opportunity.

Illuminating the Shadow

In Jungian psychology, the "shadow" is part of the unconscious mind consisting of repressed weaknesses, shortcomings and instincts. "Everyone carries a shadow," Jung wrote, "and the less it is embodied in the individual's conscious life, the blacker and denser it is."[91] According to Jung, the shadow is instinctive and irrational and is prone to projection: turning a personal inferiority into a perceived deficiency in *someone else*. These projections prevent one from owning their own negative characteristics and make it increasingly difficult to see that one's problems may be, in fact, originating within one's self.

In a recent conversation, my friend and colleague, Cynthia Cavalli commented that "It is a wise leader who is familiar with the dynamics and complexities of the Shadow."[92] This knowledge is essential to *Sacred Leadership*, and can help leaders avoid being caught in the traps that shadow can set, i.e. thinking that upon reaching high level leadership positions the rules don't apply to them, or that they can get away with things that other people cannot.

Jon Kabat-Zinn wrote, "Not only do we not see what is there. Often we see what is not there."[93] This is the case with shadow; we see something in the other person that is not there. When someone who irritates you crosses your path, as they inevitably will, stop to ponder why and ask if you are looking at this person as a screen on which you can project your own shadow. Truly whole leaders learn to recognize that what has been activated is shadow content from their own personalities and the feeling of irritation has more to do with them than anyone else.

Leaders aware of their shadow say, "I made a mistake. I'm not perfect. I need help. It has to be 'we' not me. We will work together." They take criticism and even ask for it and are willing to change course based on the advice of others. *Sacred Leadership* recognizes that even when we think we're acting from our highest good, we may be overlooking something critical. Leaders ask others to reflect back to them what they see when they observe the leader in action. By becoming familiar with their own shadow, leaders can discern when someone else is telling them about their own shadows or projecting theirs onto them.[94]

Shadow can be personal, belonging to an individual, but societies also have a shadow, and usually it's the poor and underprivileged of those societies who end up being blamed for society's ills.

There are several instances that come to mind. The history of enslavement of African-Americans in the United States is a prime example. It has been nearly 150 years since slavery was abolished following the Civil War. Yet in many families, the pain and trauma of that experience has been passed down from one generation to another, influencing their view of the present and exerting a lasting effect on their efforts to create a better future. Likewise, many Caucasians still harbor fear and hatred of African-Americans, many times borne of their own sense of inferiority, which they project onto black Americans.

For example, in my first principalship described earlier, the staff, students and community had bought into a story based upon the shadow cast by ethnic distrust and stereotypes. As a new principal, I had to identify that shadow, shine a light on it and show that a different future was possible. Slowly, as I enlisted and engaged others, a new story emerged. It was a more positive story of hope and success. The power of the old story, shaped by shadow, began to diminish over the three years I was assigned to this school. However, the old story and the shadow it cast never completely disappeared, because some people were unable to let go of it. They had woven the thread of that old story tightly into the tapestry of their own lives.

In most leadership situations, there is some form of individual or organizational shadow that limits the possibilities into which the organization can grow and thrive. This shadow inhibits the change process and interferes with the realization of potential. In spite of those who can't let go of shadow and the old story, leaders need only remember that they do not have to enlist everyone. Only a small but crucial few need be enlisted for the shadow to begin to fade away and the new story to take hold in a powerful way.

This skill of identifying the shadow, articulating and shining a light on it, combined with the skill of framing and communicating a story of possibility, is key to transforming individuals, organizations, cultures and societies.

Dialogue

Dialogue is a simple word, but a powerful tool in the practice of *Sacred Leadership*. Dialogue is derived from the ancient Greek *dia logos* – "through words." I use the term more broadly, in that we listen with all of our senses and not just to the words.

Throughout this book, I have provided examples where dialogue led the way out of anger and hostility and onto a positive path. Adam Kahane, in his book *Solving Tough Problems: An Open Way of Talking,*

Listening, and Creating New Realities, describes how he and others used dialogue as a key tool in the reconciliation that followed the end of apartheid in South Africa, the genocide in Guatemala and many other "hot spots" throughout the world.[95] If dialogue can be effective in these extreme situations, certainly it can be a useful and powerful tool in our daily lives as leaders.

The key to dialogue is listening. Below are several suggestions for improving your skill at dialogue, including some mentioned in earlier chapters that are worth repeating:

1. Stop Talking – you can't listen if you are speaking.
2. Listen to understand. This also means quieting the "voice in your head."
3. Listen between the spaces. What are the speaker's body language, tone of voice and other non-verbal cues communicating? Are they consistent with the words being spoken?
4. What's not being said?
5. Ask questions to clarify. Rephrase the speaker's comments to show you are listening and understanding. Ask if you are understanding correctly and if there is more the speaker would like to say.
6. Be conscious of your own state of being. What prejudices, preconceived notions and emotions are coloring your understanding of what you are hearing?
7. Listen empathetically.
8. Wait before you speak. Don't interrupt.
9. When you do speak, do so to be understood, not to make a point or rebut another's point of view. Communicate not only what you're thinking, but also your feelings and what you want or need.
10. Make sure everyone is being heard and has an opportunity to participate.[96]

Finally, I would like to add, "Don't take yourself so damned seriously,"[97] which Ben Zander describes in his book, *The Art of Possibility.* Although our work may be serious, we don't need to get our egos involved by taking ourselves so seriously.

Dialogue connects us at a human level. It touches that need in all of us to not only be heard, but to also be understood. Carl Rogers put it poignantly:

> *When a person realizes he has been deeply heard, his eyes moisten. I think in some real sense, he is weeping for joy. It is as though he were saying, "Thank god, somebody heard me. Someone knows what it's like to be me."*[98]

Dialogue opens not only the mind but also the heart, allowing us to relate to one another both intellectually and emotionally, thereby developing empathic understanding.

Moral Courage

It may seem odd to list courage as a key attribute of *Sacred Leadership,* but I consider it critical. Personal courage comes in two forms, physical and moral. United States Senator and 2008 Republican presidential candidate John McCain wrote, "Courage is not the absence of fear, but the capacity for action despite our fears."[99] Courage is consciously taking action that goes beyond self-interest and self-preservation.

Physical courage is putting our lives or limbs on the line for something or someone in which we believe. With some exceptions (i.e. firefighters, police, military personnel), few of us are called upon to exhibit physical courage, although we never know when we may encounter a situation that will require it.

On the other hand, moral courage is a fundamental attribute of *Sacred Leadership.* The U. S. Army has defined moral courage as

> *…the willingness to stand firm on your values, principles and convictions – even when threatened. It enables leaders to stand up for*

what they believe is right, regardless of the consequences. Leaders, who take responsibility for their decisions and actions, even when things go wrong, display moral courage. Courageous leaders are willing to look critically inside themselves, consider new ideas and change what needs changing....Consistent moral courage is every bit as important as momentary physical courage. Situations requiring physical courage are rare; situations requiring moral courage can occur frequently.[100]

Robert Kennedy described moral courage in his *Day of Affirmation Address* at Cape Town University in South Africa.

Few men are willing to brave the disapproval of their fellows, the censure of their colleagues, the wrath of their society. Moral courage is a rarer commodity than bravery in battle or great intelligence. Yet it is the one essential, vital quality for those who seek to change the world – which yields most painfully to change.[101]

Many of the scandals that have occurred over the past two decades have reflected failures of leadership and a lack of moral courage. Leaders refused accountability and to take responsibility for the results of their actions. They failed to follow consistent values and the rule of law. Those who practice *Sacred Leadership* exhibit moral courage both personally and professionally. As I mentioned earlier in the book, they must do the right things right, and for the right reasons.

Moral courage requires candor and frankness. It may mean delivering "bad" news to your boss or refusing to carry out a directive that is illegal or inconsistent with your values or the organization's mission.

On a daily basis, as well as in the midst of chaos, *Sacred Leadership* requires that we act in a manner consistent with our values and mission to serve the greatest good now and in the future. Leaders display moral courage even when their actions may result in negative consequences for them personally or professionally. There is no easy way out. Anything less is not *Sacred Leadership*.

Collaborative Competence

Sacred Leadership is a collaborative process. It requires enlisting, engaging and sustaining the involvement of others, what Otto Scharmer calls collaborative competence.[102] Each group, community or organization is unique and requires specific and often different techniques in building collaboration.

The leader must know how to guide a group in a collaborative process that helps fulfill the stated mission. The first step in this process is becoming comfortable with yourself – to accept and connect with who you are individually and as a member of the group. Only then can you successfully help others move through the collaborative process and into the possibilities and outcomes they want to emerge.

Another key role of the leader is to facilitate the collaborative competence of others. *Sacred Leadership* requires one to be a skilled facilitator of group interaction. Leadership and facilitation of the group process should be shared as the group's competence grows. Only when the group gains this competence can the leader expect the work to be sustainable.[103]

Resilience and Perseverance

I'll conclude with the attributes of resilience and perseverance. Whenever we are in a leadership position, we are bound to encounter obstacles and setbacks, some of which can be very stressful and even traumatic. During these times leaders must display resilience and practice perseverance.

Resilience is the ability to positively adapt to adversity, trauma and other significant stressors. Many describe resilience as simply the ability to "bounce back" from difficult situations. Perseverance, on the other hand, is the ability to continue to move forward as we are "bouncing back" from adversity. We maintain forward momentum towards achieving our mission in spite of the difficulties we are facing. Resilience and perseverance work hand in hand and are absolutely essential for the practice of *Sacred Leadership*.

Most studies have found that caring and supportive relationships are a key component of maintaining resilience. Resilient leaders have a core group of trusted and understanding people they can reach out to for support in difficult times. Supportive relationships take time to develop, so leaders must build and nurture this network throughout their careers, long before adversity strikes. They may be friends, family or professional colleagues. I have been fortunate throughout my life to find support from each of these groups. For example, think back to those four teachers that greeted me in the faculty cafeteria that first morning when I walked into John Adams Junior High School. They became a cornerstone of my resilience throughout my first year of teaching.

Below I have adapted and summarized a list of ten ways to build resilience as outlined in the pamphlet, *The Road to Resilience,* published by the American Psychological Association.[104]

- *Make connections* – good relationships and a willingness to accept help and support from those who care about you strengthens resilience.
- *Avoid seeing crises as insurmountable problems* – you can't change the fact that bad things happen, but you can change how you interpret and respond to them.
- *Accept that change is a part of living* – focus on those things over which you have influence or control.
- *Move toward your goals* – develop realistic goals and regularly take small steps toward achieving them.
- *Take decisive actions* – do something, rather than wishing the problem will just go away.

- *Look for opportunities for self-discovery* – identify ways in which the adversity has helped you grow and learn.
- *Nurture a positive view of yourself* – have confidence in your abilities and trust your instincts.
- *Keep things in perspective* – don't blow things out of proportion.
- *Maintain a hopeful outlook* – be optimistic and visualize what you want rather than focusing on your fear.
- *Take care of yourself* – pay attention to your own emotional needs and feelings. Take care of your physical well-being through exercise, healthful eating and maintaining appropriate sleep patterns.

It is important to remember that in the midst of adversity and chaos, the organization is watching the way leaders respond. *Sacred Leadership* recognizes that colleagues and followers will pick up on and mirror the leader's attitudes and actions, good or bad. Once the situation has stabilized, or even before it has done so, the leader must persevere, set the standard and begin the movement forward. *Sacred Leadership* requires flexibility as the leader maintains focus on the sacred mission, honors the organization's core values and enlists and engages others as the team navigates its way through the adversity.

Remember – before we can lead others, we must first lead ourselves. These skills and attributes represent the starting point for your personal journey on the path to *Sacred Leadership*.

Chapter 7 Questions for Reflection

1. Do you have the requisite management skills and emotional intelligence to lead? How do you know?

2. Of the nine skills and attributes outlined in this chapter, which are your strongest? Think of specific examples of times when you have used them. How did their use make a difference in the outcomes?

3. How do you maintain high levels of self-awareness on a day-to-day basis?

4. How do you find stillness? Do you effectively create a gap so you are not pressured into premature decision-making? If not, what can you do to improve?

5. When has your intuition served your leadership? When was the last time that you experienced a synchronistic event?

6. Are you aware of your "shadow"? What does it look like? How does it show itself?

7. How can you improve your skills of dialogue? How would you rate yourself on a scale of 1-10?

8. When was the last time you displayed "moral courage"? Has there been a recent time when you did not display "moral courage" even though you should have?

9. How skilled are you at collaborative competence? How are you facilitating the collaborative competence of your team?

10. How are you nurturing your resilience? When was the last time you persevered against what seemed to be unbeatable odds?

11. What is your plan to further develop these skills and attributes?

EPILOGUE

Throughout this book, I expressed my belief that we stand at a transitional point in our development as a nation and as human beings. The issues we face hold global implications for the kind of world future generations will inherit.

We can choose to see our choices as a portal into a positive future that is full of possibility born of human imagination, creativity and interconnectedness. Or, we can let that portal close and turn back into the past, wallowing in the mire of hatred born of self-centeredness and superstition – a set of conditions not unlike the Dark Ages.[105]

For me, the choice is clear and my focus is the future. I am optimistic. My optimism springs from the fact that we have a choice and with choice comes possibility.

I'd Love to Change the World

I'd Love to Change the World is a hit song by the 1960s blues rock group Ten Years After. In the tune, lead singer Alvin Lee sang, "I'd love to change the world/ but I don't know what to do/ so I'll leave it up to you."[106]

To participate in *Sacred Leadership*, one *cannot* leave choice up to another. *Sacred Leadership* is a collective experience, requiring each individual to respond to his or her chosen mission to serve the greatest good.

In the current leadership paradigm, we trust our political, business and religious leaders to guide us through chaotic and transitional times – we leave it up to them. Sometimes, they hit a home run. Most often, they only smack a base hit, then leave us stranded on the bases after the game has ended. At other times, they strike out.

Today, many don't even show up for the game.

Sacred Leadership represents the new paradigm in which each of us can bring our own understanding, gifts and talents in full support of the greatest good. It is a call to a consciousness of the greatest good and the need for sustainability. We can no longer rest or sleep while leaving it up to others to sustain our cause or purpose. Each of us must cultivate the ability to clearly and openly hold a space of awareness so others may awake to contribute to their own sacred mission.

Be the Change

Our old leadership paradigm is no longer effective in this new world. Rather than abdicate our responsibility and assume ourselves to be victims of the incompetence and corruptness of our leaders, we can choose to step up in our daily personal and professional lives through our practice of *Sacred Leadership*. We need to display the moral courage to share our dreams and aspirations for a positive future and demand a focus on the greatest good and the long-term, sustainable well-being of the planet. We need to leave our cynicism behind.

Sacred Leadership requires that we stand up and use our gifts and talents in service to the greatest good. We accomplish this one interaction at a time.

We need to start talking to one another and, more importantly, listening to one another. We wake up each day to our individual stories about the kind of world in which we live and the kind of future we want to create. We enact those stories as we greet our friends and families over breakfast, interact with the bus driver on the way to work, or speak with our co-workers throughout the day.

Sacred Leadership does not give us a pass "to leave it up to you." In his book *The Divine Matrix*, author Gregg Braden put it this way:

146

"One person must choose a new way of being and live that difference in the presence of others so that it can be seen and sealed into their pattern."[107] Those who practice *Sacred Leadership* not only see that new way of being; they choose to live it in their daily lives in the presence of their family, friends and colleagues.

Each of us can "choose a new way of being" and "live that difference in the presence of others" by beginning the journey of *Sacred Leadership* right now:

- As leaders in the service professions, recommit to your mission and align your mission and values to serving the greatest good and a sustainable future.
- As business leaders, talk with your employees about their dreams and aspirations. How does working for you help them achieve their personal and professional goals –an alignment that benefits everyone?
- As political leaders, take the long view and focus on the greatest good. How can you articulate what you stand for rather than what you're against?
- As parents, impart positive values and respect for the greatest good to your children; listen to and nurture your children's dreams and aspirations.
- As religious leaders, live your faiths while respecting those who believe differently. How can you build upon our commonalities rather than emphasizing our differences? How can you use the positive force of religion to serve those in need and the greatest good?

Through each of these interactions we become the possibility we want to emerge in the world. Big changes grow out of these small interactions as they create a virtuous cycle.

A Call to Action

I close the book by returning to the practice of moral courage. The word courage is derived from the Latin, *cor*, which has come to mean heart. Throughout the book I have written about the need to have an open heart. An open heart implies vulnerability, and requires moral courage.

To practice *Sacred Leadership* one must speak from the heart. This is difficult for many and especially difficult in a world in which cynicism is not only acceptable, it is even celebrated. We must, however, have the courage to speak about the sacred nature of our work; about our belief that there is a greater good that can be achieved; that there are a set of core values that we, as a society, can agree upon and practice; and that we can provide a better future for our children.

As I have spoken about *Sacred Leadership* over the past few years, I have sometimes been called naïve, or a Pollyanna; yet I cannot let these voices stop me from pursuing this new way of leading, nor can you. We all must exhibit the moral courage to speak from our hearts and look for those who resonate with our message. It is with these people that *Sacred Leadership* will emerge.

Join the Conversation and the Journey at:
www.sacredleadership.org

END NOTES

[1] In Chapter 3 I discuss how the concept of "common good" evolved into the principle of the "greatest good."

[2] Heilemann, John and Mark Halperin, *Game Change: Obama and the Clintons, McCain and Palin, and the Race of a Lifetime,* (Harper Collins Publishers: NY, 2010) (Electronic Kindle Edition location 382-88).

[3] "The State of Corporate Citizenship: A View from Inside," (Boston College, Center for Corporate Citizenship: Boston, November 11, 2005).

[4] "The State of Corporate Citizenship 2009: Weathering the Storm," (Boston College, Center for Corporate Citizenship: Boston, September 22, 2009).

[5] Lifsher, Marc, "Firms file for do-good status" *Los Angeles Times*, January 4, 2012, p. B4.

[6] Supreme Court of The United States, *Citizens United v. Federal Election Commission*, Appeal From The United States District Court For The District of Columbia, (No. 08–205. Argued March 24, 2009 – Reargued September 9, 2009 – Decided January 21, 2010) This opinion can be found at: http://www.supremecourt.gov/opinions/09pdf/08-205.pdf

[7] Definition of sacred from the Merriam-Webster online dictionary at (http://www.merriam-webster.com/dictionary/sacred).

[8] Zohar, Danah and Marshall, Ian, *Spiritual Capital – Wealth We Can Live By*, (Berrett-Koehler Publishers, Inc.: San Francisco, 2004), p. 3.

[9] Tom Hanks narrates the epic story of the 9/11 boatlift that evacuated half a million people from the stricken piers and seawalls

of Lower Manhattan. Produced and directed by Eddie Rosen-stein. Eyepop Productions, Inc. You can view this documentary film at (http://youtube/181sxFcDrjo). BOATLIFT was executive produced by Stephen Flynn and Sean Burke, and co-directed by Rich Velleu. It premiered on September 8th at the 9/11 Tenth Anniversary Summit: Remembrance/Renewal/Resilience in Washington D.C. The film was made with the generous support by philanthropist Adrienne Arsht, Chairman Emerita, TotalBank (www.arsht.com).

10   Kelly, Eamonn, *Powerful Times – Rising to the Challenge of Our Uncertain World,* (Wharton School Publishing: New Jersey, 2006) p. 46.

11   Kelley, p. 47.

12   Throughout the ages it has been said that these are times like no other. However, the convergence of communication, computing, biological and nano technology at exponential rates has indeed created a time of choice like no other.

13   Otto Scharmer provides a detailed understanding of this move-ment from open mind, to open heart, to open will in his book *Theory U – Leading from the Future as It Emerges*, (Society for Organizational Learning: Cambridge, MA, 2007) This form of thinking draws heavily from the Buddhist traditions.

14   Scharmer, C. Otto, *Theory U – Leading from the Future as It Emerges*, (Society for Organizational Learning: Cambridge, MA, 2007) pp. 399-401. A discussion of the "voice in the head" is also found in Ben Zander's video *Leadership: an Art of Possibility*, produced by Groh Productions, 2005.

15   Emerson, Ralph Waldo, Essays, 1841. Quoted in *The Oxford Dictionary of Quotations, Fifth Edition,* edited by Elizabeth Knowles, (Oxford University Press: Oxford, England, 1999) p. 299:20. The actual quote is, "All history becomes subjective; in

other words there is properly no history, only biography." *The Essays of Ralph Waldo Emerson,* (Easton Press: Norwalk, Connecticut, 1979) p. 5.

[16] Mitchell, Edgar, Apollo 14 Astronaut quoted at www.dailygood.org.

[17] Aristotle, *Politics & Poetics,* Translated by Benjamin Jowett in 1964, (Easton Press: Norwalk, Connecticut, 1979), p. 84.

[18] Declaration of Independence of the United States of America.

[19] Constitution of the United States of America.

[20] *Faith and Progressive Policy Initiative*, Center for American Progress, conducted by Financial Dynamics, 2006.

[21] Senge, Peter, Scharmer, C. Otto, Jaworski, Joseph, & Flowers, Betty Sue Flowers, *Presence: Human Purpose and the Field of the Future,* (Society for Organizational Learning: Cambridge, MA, 2004) p. 223.

[22] Ibid. p. 195.

[23] Hock, Dee, *Birth of the Chaordic Age,* (Berrett-Koehler Publishers Inc.: San Francisco, 1999), pp. 7-8.

[24] Ibid. p. 8.

[25] Brown, Juanita with Isaacs, David, *The World Café – Shaping Our Futures Through Conversations That Matter,* (Berrett-Koehler Publishers, Inc.: San Francisco, 2005).

[26] Velasquez, Manuel, Andre, Claire, et. al., "The Common Good," at http://www.scu.edu/ethics/practicing/decision/commongood. html, originally putlished in *Ethics*, V5 N1 (Spring 1992).

[27] Ibid.

[28] Ibid.

[29] Ibid.

[30] Ibid.

[31] Etzioni, Amitai, March 2005 Blog Post, "Educating for Freedom and Responsibility."

32 Velasquez, et.al.

33 Appiah, Kwame Anthony, *Cosmopolitanism, Ethics in a World of Strangers,* (W. W. Norton & Company, Inc: New York, NY, 2006) p. xii.

34 King, Jr., Martin Luther, "Discovering Lost Values," a sermon delivered to the Second Baptist Church in Detroit Michigan on February 28, 1954. A transcript of this sermon can be found at http://mlkkpp01.stanford.edu/primarydocuments/Vol2/540228 RediscoveringLostValues.pdf.

35 I recognize that not all values are positive; however, in the context of *Sacred Leadership* I assume that the values we discuss are positive in nature.

36 Sullivan, Gordon and Harper, Michael, *Hope is Not a Method.* (Broadway Books: New York, 1996), p. 63, quoted in Hannon, Nanci, "A Study of the Effect of Organizational Culture on Leadership Practices within Defense Agencies, "(U.S. Army War College, Carlisle Barracks, Pennsylvania. April 10, 2000).

37 *Army Leadership – Be Know, Do, Field Manual No. 22-100,* (Headquarters, Department of the Army, Washington D.C., August 31, 1999).

38 The structure of this discussion about the role of values has been adapted from the work of John Maxwell *The 17 Indisputable Laws of Teamwork Workbook,* (Thomas Nelson Publishers, Inc.: Nashville, 2003) pp. 159-161.

39 Sullivan, Gordon and Harper, Michael, *Hope is Not a Method.* (Broadway Books: New York, 1996), p.64, quoted in Hannon, Nanci, "A Study of the Effect of Organizational Culture on Leadership Practices within Defense Agencies," (U.S. Army War College, Carlisle Barracks, Pennsylvania. April 10, 2000).

40 Lencioni, Patrick, *The Five Dysfunctions of a Team.* (San Francisco: Jossey Bass – A Wiley Imprint: San Francisco, 2002) p.

188.

⁴¹ Kusy, Mitchell & Holloway, Elizabeth, "Cultivating a Culture of Respectful Engagement," *Leader to Leader* (Number 58: Fall, 2010) p. 52.

⁴² Sergiovanni, Thomas J., *Moral Leadership – Getting to the Heart of School Improvement,* (Jossey-Bass: San Francisco, 1998) p. 21.

⁴³ Gallup Organization. Survey conducted for the Princeton Religion Research Center, Princeton, N.J., March 11-20, 1988, reported in, Sergiovanni, Thomas J., *Moral Leadership – Getting to the Heart of School Improvement,* (Jossey-Bass: San Francisco, 1998) p. 21.

⁴⁴ Marquand, Robert, (Staff writer), "Phone hacking letter spells more trouble for Murdoch and News Corp," *The Christian Science Monitor*: August 16, 2011.

⁴⁵ Finkelstein, Sydney, Whitehead, Jo and Campbell, Andrew. "What Drives Leaders to Make Bad Decisions," *Leader to Leader*, Number 53 – Summer, 2009. (Jossey-Bass: New York) p. 52.

⁴⁶ Ibid. p 54.

⁴⁷ There are many values inventories available. A free online values inventory can be found at www.lifevaluesinventory.org. I recommend that you try several and determine the one that best fits you.

⁴⁸ Mead, Margaret, I have been unable to locate when and where this quote was first cited. The Institute for Intercultural Studies believes it probably came into circulation through a newspaper report of something said spontaneously and informally. They maintain, however, that it was firmly rooted in her professional work and that it reflected a conviction that she expressed often, in different contexts and phrasings. See http://www.interculturalstudies.org.

⁴⁹ Gilmartin, Ray, "After The Turmoil: Former Merck CEO Says

Execs Need New Beliefs" at (http://www.forbes.com/sites/edsilverman/2011/09/27/after-the-turmoil-former-merck-ceo-says-execs-need-new-beliefs/) September 27, 2011.

50 Personal interview and review of internal document entitled "The Either Effect." The CEO requested that he and his company remain anonymous.

51 Kahane Adam, *Solving Tough Problems,* (Berrett-Koehler Publishers, Inc.: San Francisco, 2004). p. 32.

52 Brown, Juanita and Isaacs, David, *The World Café – Shaping Our Futures Through Conversations That Matter,* (Berrett-Koehler Publishers, Inc.: San Francisco, 2005).

53 Fluker, Walter Earl, "Leading Ethically at the Intersection Where Worlds Collide," *Leader to Leader*, Number 54, Fall 2009, p. 32.

54 Ibid., p. 35.

55 Collins, Jim, *Good To Great* (Harper Collins Publishers, Inc.: New York, 2001) p. 41.

56 Block, Peter, *Community – The Structure of Belonging,* (Berrett-Koehler Publishers, Inc.: San Francisco, 2008) p. 88.

57 Toffler, Alvin, *Future Shock,* (Bantam Books/Random House, Inc.: New York, 1970) p. 9.

58 Millett, Stephen M., "Five Principles of Futuring as Applied History," *The Futurist*, September-October, 2011, p. 41.

59 Strategic Foresight is becoming widely used. I recently attended a weeklong seminar on Strategic Foresight. There were representatives from the corporate world, law enforcement, immigration agencies, non-profit organizations and the medical field participating. Many of these organizations had already established internal Strategic Foresight positions and departments,

60 Hines, Andy & Bishop, Peter, editors, *Thinking About the Future: Guidelines for Strategic Foresight,* (Social Technologies, LLC: Washington D.C., 2006). Also note that the editors are faculty in

the Futures Studies program at the University of Houston which offers certificates and degrees in strategic foresight.

[61] Herbert, Frank, *Dune,* (Berkley Books: New York, 1981) p. 40.

[62] Aristotle. *The Nicomachean Ethics, Book Six.* Trans. J.A. K. Thomson 1953. (Easton Press: Norwalk, Connecticut, 1999) (The original was writtend around 334 BC).

[63] Hayashi, Alden M., "When to Trust Your Gut," *Harvard Business Review*, February 2001, p 60.

[64] Ibid., p. 61.

[65] Bruner, Robert, "Professor Says Business Schools and Students Can Take Away Lessons From Financial Crisis," *Wall Street Journal*, August 20, 2009, p. B5.

[66] An interview with William Gibson on *Talk of the Nation* (National Public Radio: November 30, 1999).

[67] Eagleman, David, *Incognito, The Secret Lives of Brains,* (Pantheon Books: New York, 2011) p. 8.

[68] In the book *Endophysics, Time, Quantum and the Subjective,* Paul Bernstein highlights that for at least 100 years, scientists have been studying forms of intuition under controlled laboratory conditions. He goes on to say that in practice the focus has been on three types of intuition: telepathy – information which we gain from another person; remote viewing – information which we gain about another place or object; and precognition and presentiment which is information we gain about the future. For the purposes of this chapter, I am referring to intuition as pre-cognition and presentiment. I have not discussed any of the other forms of intuition in detail because the research has yet to be accepted by the scientific establishment. For those who would like to learn more, I suggest the readings described above as well as Dean Radin's book *Entangled Minds,* (Paraview: New York, 2006).

[69] Greenleaf, Robert K., *The Servant as Leader,* (The Greenleaf Center for Servant Leadership, Westfield, IN, 2008) p. 23 (The original essay was published in 1970).

[70] Ibid., p. 25.

[71] Smarr, Larry, personal interview.

[72] Kabat-Zinn, Jon, *Coming to Our Senses – Healing Ourselves and the World Through Mindfulness,* (Hyperion: New York, 2005) pp. 148-149.

[73] Dreher, Diane, *The Tao of Inner Peace,* (Penguin Putnam, Inc.: New York, 2000) pp. 87-88. This book provides many simple exercises and affirmations.

[74] Kabat-Zinn, Jon, *Coming to Our Senses – Healing Ourselves and the World Through Mindfulness,* (Hyperion: New York, 2005). This book is an excellent source for those interested in Mindful Meditation.

[75] Seeing your seeing comes from a variety of mindfulness perspectives. See Jung, Scharmer, and Kabat-Zinn referenced above.

[76] Edward De Bono's notion of "water logic," provides a simple tool that takes us beyond the knowing of the immediate *"this"* (*"this"* is a pencil – a space of knowing), to a space of learning by routinely asking questions like "What will *'this'* lead to?" and "Where did *'this'* come from?" A brief description of "water logic can be found on Edward De Bono's website at (http://www.edwdebono.com/ debono/wl.htm).

[77] Tracy Houston provides some interesting methods for improving what I call "Deep Listening" in her book *Inside Out: Stores and Methods for Generating Collective Will to Create the Future We Want,* (Society for Organizational Learning, Inc.: Cambridge, MA, 2007).

[78] Hayashi, Alden M., "When to Trust Your Gut," *Harvard Business Review,* February 2001, p 63.

⁷⁹ Jaworski, Joseph, *Synchronicity: The Inner Path of Leadership*, (Berrett-Koehler Publishers: San Francisco, 1998) p. 182.

⁸⁰ As quoted in "Arun Gandhi Shares the Mahatma's Message" by Michel W. Potts, in *India – West* (San Leandro, California) Vol. XXVII, No. 13 (1 February 2002) p. A34; Arun Gandhi indirectly quoting his grandfather. See also. "Be the change you wish to see: An interview with Arun Gandhi" by Carmella B'Hahn, *Reclaiming Children and Youth* [Bloomington] Vol.10, No. 1 (Spring 2001) p. 6. No evidence he ever said this see: Morton, Brian (August 29, 2011). "Falser Words Were Never Spoken." *NY Times*. From (http://en.wikiquote.org/wiki/Mohandas_Karamchand_Gandhi).

⁸¹ I do not mean to downplay the importance of emotional intelligence in the context of leadership. A great deal has been written about this topic and I have chosen not to review this work here. I recommend the following resources for those who are interested in learning more: Goleman, Daniel, *Emotional Intelligence: Why it can matter more than IQ*, (Bantam Books: New York, October 1995); Goleman, Daniel, "What Makes a Leader?," *Harvard Business Review*, January 2004 (originally published in 1998), pp. 82-91; Goleman, Daniel, Boyatzis, Richard and McKee, Annie, *Primal Leadership: Realizing the Power of Emotional Intelligence*, (Harvard Business School Press: Boston, Massachusetts, 2002); and Goleman, Daniel, *Leadership: The Power of Emotional Intelligence*, (More Than Sound LLC: Northampton, Massachusetts, 2011).

⁸² Appiah, Kwame Anthony, *Cosmopolitanism*, (W. W. Norton & Company: New York, 2006) p.170.

⁸³ Lennick, Dough & Kiel, Fred, "Moral Intelligence for Successful Leadership," *Leader to Leader*, #40, Spring 2006, p. 13-16.

⁸⁴ Kabat-Zinn, Jon, *Coming to Our Senses – Healing Ourselves and*

the World Through Mindfulness, (Hyperion: New York, 2005) p. 11.

85 Tolle, Eckhart, *A New Earth: Awakening to Your Life's Purpose,* (Dutton: New York, 2005) p. 32.

86 Kabat-Zinn, p. 46.

87 Rifkin, Jeremy, *The Empathic Civilization,* (The Penguin Group: New York, 2009) p. 10.

88 Hoffman, Martin referenced in Goleman, Daniel, *Emotional Intelligence,* (Bantam Books: New York, 1995) p. 105.

89 Rifkin, p. 37.

90 Campbell, Joseph, Editor, *The Portable Jung,* (Penguin Books: New York, 1971) p. 505.

91 Jung, C.G. (1938). "Psychology and Religion." In *CW 11: Psychology and Religion: West and East.* p. 131.

92 This discussion of "shadow" is based upon personal correspondence with Cynthia Cavalli, a doctoral student at Fielding Graduate University, November 14, 2011.

93 Kabat-Zinn, p. 44.

94 This discussion of "shadow" is based upon personal dialogue and correspondence with Cynthia Cavalli, a doctoral student at Fielding Graduate University. Many of the ideas expressed are drawn from that correspondence and are used with her permission. Additional, information was drawn from *The Portable Jung,* edited by Joseph Campbell (Viking Penguin Press: New York, 1971) pp. 139-162.

95 Kahane, Adam, *Solving Tough Problems: An Open Way of Talking, Listening and Creating New Realities,* (Berrett-Koehler Publishers, Inc.: San Francisco, 2004) p. 3.

96 This list has been adapted from Rick Ross, "Skillful Discussion: Protocols for Reaching a Decision Mindfully," in Peter M. Senge et al. *The Fifth Discipline Fieldbook: Strategies and Tools for Building*

a Learning Organization (Doubleday/Currency: New York, 1994) p. 391. It also draws upon the general tools of active listening.

⁹⁷ Zander, Rosamund Stone, & Zander, Ben, *The Art of Possibility*, (Penguin Books: New York, 2000) p. 79.

⁹⁸ Rogers, Carl R. "Reinhold Niebuhr's *The Self and the Dramas of History*: A Criticism." *Pastoral Psychology*, (Volume 9, #6), September, 1958, pp. 15-17. Quoted in *The Empathic Civilization*, p. 14.

⁹⁹ McCain, John with Salter, Mark, *Why Courage Matters*, (Random House, Inc.: New York, 2004) p. 9.

¹⁰⁰ *Army Leadership: Be, Know, Do, Field Manual No. 22-100*, (Headquarters, Department of the Army: Washington, D. C., 1999) pp. 2-9.

¹⁰¹ Kennedy, Robert F., "A Tiny Ripple of Hope" Day of Affirmation Address at Cape Town University, South Africa, delivered June 6, 1966. An audio recording of this speech can be heard at (http://www.americanrhetoric.com/speeches/rfkcapetown.htm).

¹⁰² Scharmer, Otto, "Ten propositions on transforming the current leadership development paradigm," a paper prepared for – Round Table Meeting on Leadership For Development Impact, The World Bank, (The World Bank Institute: Washington, D.C., September 27-28, 2009). Scharmer uses the term "collaborative competence" in this paper.

¹⁰³ There are hundreds of books written about specific facilitation and group process techniques that one can reference. I strongly suggest that the reader participate in facilitation training to hone their skills.

¹⁰⁴ *The Road to Resilience*, American Psychological Association, (http://www.apa.org/helpcenter/road-resilience.aspx) Retrieved January, 4, 2012. p. 2.

¹⁰⁵ I believe in looking to the past only to gather the wisdom, in

sight and experience that enable us to move forward with purpose and clarity. The past can tell us what went wrong but it cannot tell us the direction for moving into the future.

[106] "I'd Love to Change the World" written by Allen Lee, lyrics © Chrysalis Music Group.

[107] Braden, Gregg, *The Divine Matrix*, (Hay House, Inc: Carlsbad, California, 2007) p. 204.

INDEX

V

W

ABOUT THE AUTHOR

James W. Davis is the founder and President of The Davis Group Ltd, an international consulting firm specializing in leadership development and executive coaching. Mr. Davis has over 40 years of experience in the public, non-profit and private sectors.

Prior to forming his consulting practice in 1997, Mr. Davis served 27 years in a variety of leadership positions in public education including five years as Superintendent. He is the co-founder of the Institute for Educational Advancement.

Mr. Davis has also worked for Johns Hopkins University, the RAND Corporation and as an adjunct professor at the University of Southern California.

13158618R00106

Made in the USA
Charleston, SC
19 June 2012